THE
AGA KHAN
MUSEUM
TORONTO

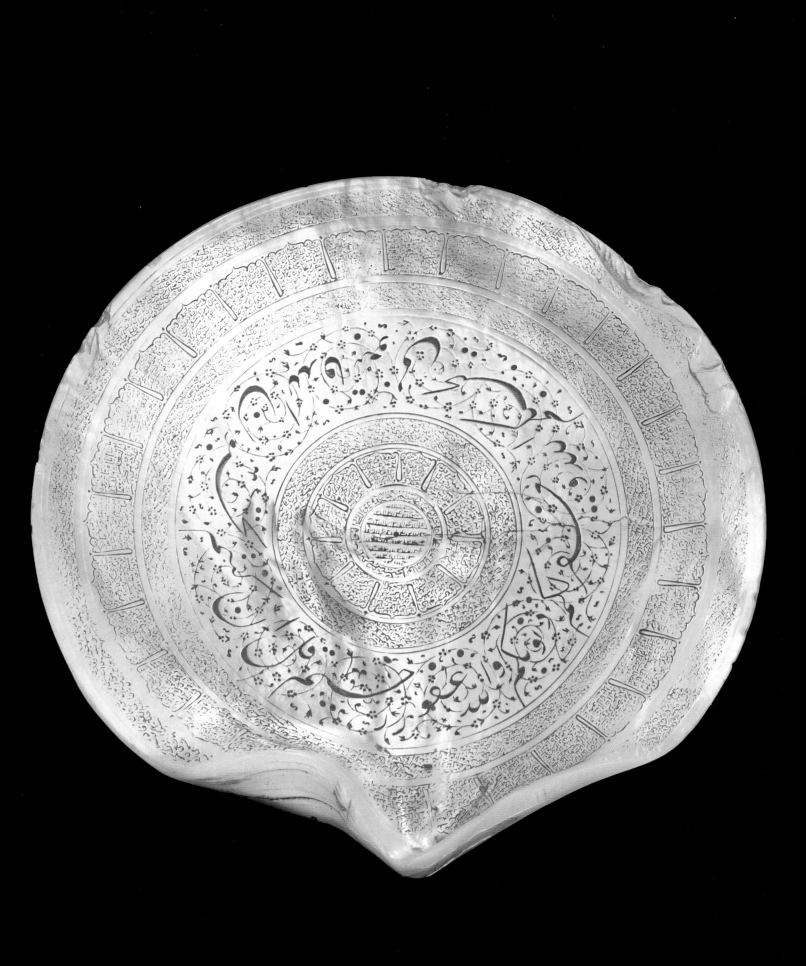

Philip Jodidio

THE
AGA KHAN
MUSEUM

TORONTO

PRESTEL   Munich · Berlin · London · New York

CONTENTS

PREFACE

His Highness the Aga Khan

No honour is like knowledge. No belief is like modesty and patience,
no attainment is like humility, no power is like forbearance,
and no support is more reliable than consultation.

Hazrat Ali ibn Abi Talib (c. 599–661)

Throughout history, and sadly even today, fear of 'the other' has torn apart communities along racial, religious, linguistic and ethnic lines. Understanding 'the other' requires a level of dialogue and knowledge which institutions such as museums can foster. Museums have a strong educational impact: they present evidence of material cultures, without intermediaries, in a direct way that appeals to people both on emotional and intellectual levels. The need to bridge the growing divide of misunderstanding between East and West is pressing and, therefore, I have chosen to establish a museum of Islamic art, the Aga Khan Museum, in Toronto, Canada.

Canada has for many years been a beacon to the rest of the world for its commitment to pluralism and its support for the multicultural richness and diversity of its peoples. It is precisely this diversity that sustains the moral and dynamic coherence in public life that Canada has so successfully constructed, and is predicated on the ethic of respect for human dignity. The country has fully embraced pluralism as a foundation for its strength and growth and I am convinced that this is absolutely necessary for the stability of an interdependent world.

The Aga Khan Museum, designed by the renowned Japanese architect Fumihiko Maki and to be built in several phases, is conceived primarily as an educational institution in the field of Islamic art and culture, a specific mandate unique in North America. It will be dedicated to presenting Islamic arts and culture in their historic, cultural and geographical diversity, with the aim of fostering knowledge and understanding both within Muslim societies and between these societies and other cultures. The search for knowledge is a fundamental aspect of the faith of Islam and has been central to the rise of Muslim civilizations. I think of the words of Hazrat Ali, the first hereditary Imam of the Shia Muslims, and the last of the four rightly guided Caliphs.

The virtues endorsed by Hazrat Ali are qualities which subordinate the self and emphasize others: modesty, patience, humility, forbearance and consultation. What he is telling us is that the best path to knowledge is to admit first what it is we do not know, and to open our minds to what others can teach us. At various times in world history, the locus of knowledge has moved from one centre of learning to another. Europe once came to the Islamic world for intellectual enrichment – and even rediscovered its own classical roots by searching in Arabic texts; therefore it is fitting that the Aga Khan Museum, an institution whose aim is to share knowledge and to educate about Muslim civilizations, will be located in Canada, a country made up of immigrants and peoples from all over the world, with different traditions and faiths sharing common values.

It is important to note that what happens in North America, culturally, economically and politically, cannot fail to have worldwide repercussions – which is why the Museum will aim to contribute to a deeper understanding among cultures and to the strengthening of cultural pluralism: essential to peace, and to progress, in our world.

The developing political crises of recent years, and the considerable lack of knowledge of the Muslim world in many Western societies, are surely related. This ignorance spans all aspects of the peoples of Islam: their pluralism, the diversity of their interpretations of the Qur'anic faith, the chronological and geographical extent of their history and culture, as well as their ethnic, linguistic and social diversity.

Many today across the Muslim world know their history and deeply value their heritage, but are also keenly sensitive to the radically altered conditions of the modern world. They also realize how erroneous and unreasonable it is to believe that there is an unbridgeable divide between their heritage and the modern world.

The need for better understanding across cultures has never been greater – or more pressing. It is important that the diversity of cultures – and the inherent pluralism that characterizes many societies today – be acknowledged as a vital asset and a prerequisite for progress and development. We must also recognize that we have a common heritage, built on centuries of cultural and commercial exchanges, and must do our utmost to value and protect what is greatest in this common humanity.

What might be the role of museums in promoting understanding between East and West? It is a very important question to which I shall not try to give a comprehensive response, but I should nevertheless point out that the Muslim world, with its history and cultures, and indeed its different interpretations of Islam, is still little known in the West. This lack of knowledge manifests itself in a particularly serious way in Western democracies, where the public is often ill-informed about the Muslim world – an ignorance which then impacts the formulation of national and international policy vis-à-vis the Muslim world. Be that as it may, Muslim and non-Muslim societies must, as a matter of urgency, make a real effort to get to know one another, for I fear that what we have is not a clash of civilizations, but a clash of ignorance on both sides. Insofar as civilizations manifest and express themselves through their art, museums have an essential role to play in teaching an understanding, respect and appreciation for other cultures and traditions and in ensuring that whole populations are given fresh opportunities to make contact with each other, using new, modern methods imaginatively and intelligently to bring about truly global communication.

The Aga Khan Museum will be a resource for the large Muslim population living in Canada and the United States. It will be a source of pride and identity, showing the inherent pluralism of Islam, not only in terms of religious interpretations but also in terms of culture and ethnicity. These aspects are important because there is no doubt whatsoever that the Muslims of North America will play an important role in their own societies and in the development of states and populations within the *umma*.

It is especially at times when ignorance, conflict and apprehension are so rife that institutions, in the Muslim world and in the West, have a greater obligation to promote intellectual openness and tolerance and to create increased cultural understanding. The Aga Khan Museum will have a unique responsibility to engender this understanding, based on a refreshed, enlightened appreciation of the scientific, linguistic, artistic and religious traditions that underpin and give such global value to Muslim civilizations. I am convinced that our ability to honour authentic symbols of pride and identity – and to share their beauty and their power with one another – can be a tremendous force for good. This is indeed my hope.

INTRODUCTION

The Aga Khan Museum: A Repository of Heritage and a Source of Inspiration

The mission of the Museum will be to make the art of Islam in all its diversity better known. It will show the multiplicity of voices with which Islam has spoken.

Prince Amyn Aga Khan

His Highness the Aga Khan, spiritual leader of the world's fifteen million Shia Ismaili Muslims, has acted and built widely since his accession to the Imamat in 1957, almost always with the clearly stated goal of improving understanding between the Muslim world and the West. His activities, from the celebrated Aga Khan Award for Architecture to the construction of Ismaili Centres in numerous countries, have sought to promote the excellence of architecture as a means to improve knowledge and understanding rather than as a goal in and of itself. Education in the broadest sense, seen for the younger generation in the creation of the Aga Khan Academies and for more advanced studies with the Aga Khan University in Karachi and the Aga Khan Program for Islamic Architecture at Harvard University and the Massachusetts Institute of Technology, has always been at the heart of his action. The future Aga Khan Museum in Toronto will focus on the arts of Islam. It is one of a number of museum projects launched recently by His Highness the Aga Khan – two other initiatives being the Museum of Historic Cairo located in Azhar Park and the Darb al-Ahmar area undergoing urban regeneration by the Aga Khan Trust for Culture (in the Egyptian capital), and the Indian Ocean Maritime Museum in Zanzibar, where the organizations grouped under the Aga Khan Development Network (AKDN) have also been active in the restoration of historic buildings, education and the promotion of tourism.

Left, a sketch by Fumihiko Maki of an elevation of the Aga Khan Museum.

Above, a rendering of the future Museum looking toward the main entrance shows how its facades tilt outward.

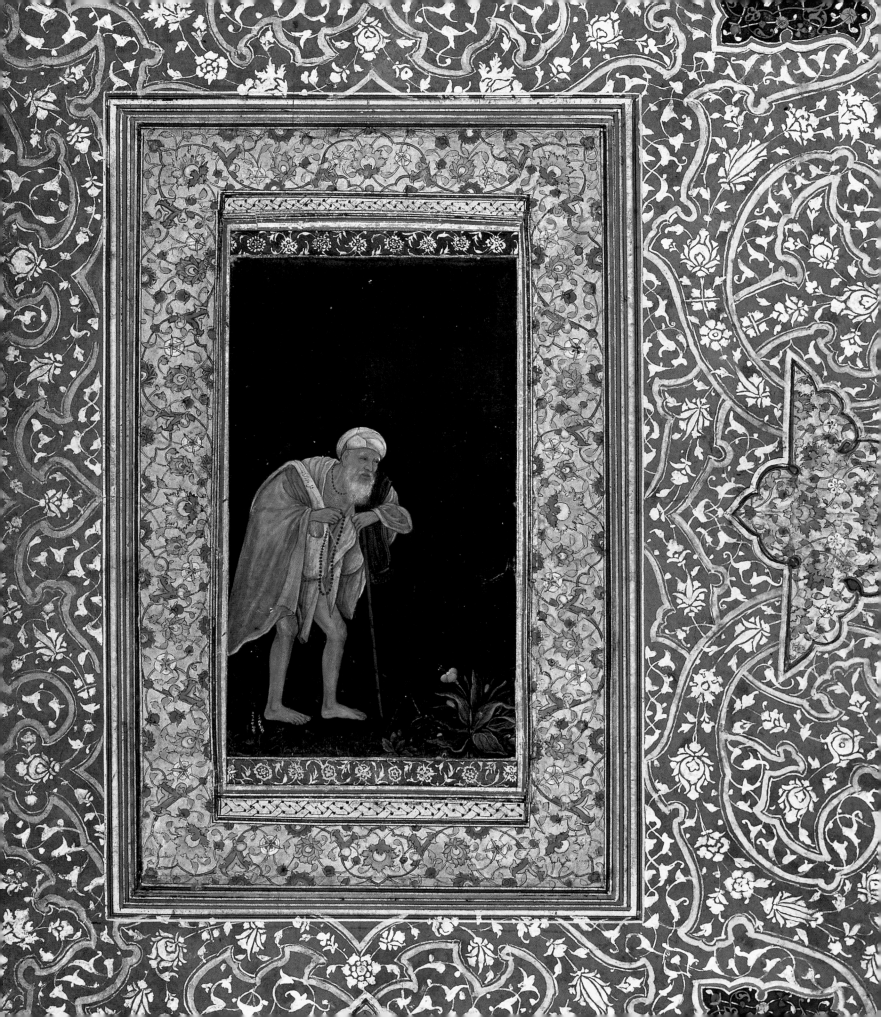

In recent years, His Highness the Aga Khan has turned considerable attention to projects in Canada. There are numerous reasons for this, but his own words best describe the motivation that has led him to announce the creation of a new museum in Toronto, as well as three other major projects. "It will not surprise you," he declared in 2006, "that I am fascinated by Canada's experience as a successful pluralistic society. My active engagement with Canada began in the 1970s when many Ismailis found a welcoming refuge here in Canada from East African ethnic strife. Since that time, the Ismaili community has planted deep roots here, become self-sufficient and can now make its own contributions to Canada's pluralistic model. That model, in turn, is one which can help to teach and inspire the entire world." With sensitivity to Canada's bilingual tradition, the Aga Khan continued this speech in French: "Comme les Canadiens le savent si bien, l'idéal du pluralisme n'est pas nouveau en ce monde. Il a des fondations honorables et anciennes, y compris des racines profondes dans la tradition islamique. Ce qui est sans précédent aujourd'hui, c'est une société mondi-alisée, intimement interconnectée et extraordinairement interdépendante."[1]

Previous double page, a rendering by Vladimir Djurovic Landscape Architecture of the garden space between the Aga Khan Museum (left) and the Ismaili Centre (right).

Left, **An Aged Pilgrim (detail)**
Miniature painting by Nadir al-Zaman'
(Abu'l Hasan)
India, Agra, c. 1618–20
Opaque watercolour and gold on paper;
11.5 × 6.5 cm
AKM 00152

Above, a rendering by Maki and Associates of an interior space in the Museum.

Two views of the Ismaili Centre (Burnaby, British Columbia, Canada; architect/planner: Bruno Freschi, 1984). The first major architectural project undertaken in Canada by His Highness the Aga Khan.

There are approximately 75,000 Ismailis in Canada, of whom 15,000 reside in the Greater Vancouver area. The first of these citizens arrived in the mid 1960s, often as students from such countries as India, Pakistan or Bangladesh (West Pakistan until 1971). The flow of Ismailis toward Canada, a country long-known for its tolerance and acceptance of the ideas of pluralism, increased in the 1970s due to conflicts in Africa and in particular the expulsion of Asians from Uganda in 1972. Though some come from Zaire, South Africa, Rwanda, Iran and Syria, a majority of Canadian Ismailis originated in Kenya, Uganda, Zanzibar and Tanzania. It was no coincidence that the first Ismaili Centre to be built in North America, designed by Bruno Freschi, was opened in Burnaby, Vancouver, in 1984.

The Aga Khan has thus undertaken to give his presence and that of his community in Canada an even more significant and symbolic turn. Two major projects in Ottawa and two in Toronto have clearly marked these initiatives. Given the importance that the Aga Khan has long placed on architecture, it should be noted that the responsibility for three of these projects has been given to two of the best-known contemporary architects in the world, Fumihiko Maki from Japan and Charles Correa from India. Maki has designed the Delegation of the Ismaili Imamat in Ottawa as well as the Aga Khan Museum in Toronto, while Correa is the architect selected to create a second Canadian Ismaili Centre, on the same Wynford Drive site in Toronto as the Museum. Both architects, as well as the landscape designer Vladimir Djurovic from Beirut, have been actively encouraged, not only by the programmatic requirements laid out for them, but also in more personal terms by the Aga Khan himself, to seek to renew the principles of the architecture of Islam in a contemporary vocabulary and in full respect for the context they are working in. When he announced the Toronto buildings in 2002, the Aga Khan stated: "In situating these two institutions in Canada, we acknowledge both a tradition of tolerance and inclusiveness as well as an environment that has permitted diversity to flourish, enriching the civic life of each individual and community that has sought to make this country its home. It is to this commitment to pluralism that we will turn in seeking to make these institutions both a repository of heritage and a source of inspiration for societies the world over in the future."[2] The fourth Canadian project today underway is the Global Centre for

Left, a summary rendering by Maki and Associates of the main approach to the Aga Khan Museum places an emphasis on its rectilinear design and outward leaning facades.

Above, a recent view of the Delegation of the Ismaili Imamat (Ottawa, Canada; design architects: Fumihiko Maki, Maki and Associates, 2008).

Pluralism, to be housed in the former Canadian War Museum in Ottawa. The Centre will seek to "produce, collect and disseminate applicable knowledge and know-how about the values, policies and practices that underpin pluralist societies."[3]

In many ways, the Aga Khan Museum, based on the arts of Islam, will be a centrepiece of all of these efforts and a truly symbolic gesture in Canada, just at the gates of the United States. Prince Amyn Aga Khan, Director of the Aga Khan Foundation, and a Director of the Aga Khan Trust for Culture, recently outlined the nature and goals of this Museum. "The mission of the Museum," he stated, "will be to make the art of Islam in all its diversity better known. It will show the multiplicity of voices with which Islam has spoken. I hope, too, that it will show something of the dialogue that has existed between the arts and the aesthetics of the non-Muslim world and the Muslim world. There is a sizeable Muslim population in North America and, indeed, in Toronto, but I think it is important that people around Toronto are better educated about Islam in general through its culture. Through that will come more understanding that will, I hope, encourage tolerance. I firmly believe that this is the right time to be creating this type of museum. I hope that many prejudices and misconceptions will be laid to rest, and through mutual understanding we will achieve mutual respect. Through mutual respect, we can hope to achieve peace."[4]

Luis Monreal, the General Manager of the Aga Khan Trust for Culture, describes the Aga Khan Museum from a slightly different perspective: "An important aspect of the strategy of His Highness over many years has indeed been to provide opportunities

Left, **Calligraphic Composition on a Sweet Chestnut Leaf**
Ottoman Turkey, 19th century
Dried chestnut leaf; 28 × 13.5 cm
AKM 00538

Above, His Highness the Aga Khan (left) in discussion with the specialist in Islamic art, Souren Melikian Chirvani, and Prince Amyn Aga Khan (right) at the exhibition of the Aga Khan Museum Collection at the Louvre, Paris, in 2007.

A rendering by Vladimir Djurovic Landscape
Architecture of part of the gardens in spring.

for the West to learn about the culture and civilization of Islam. Within this framework, he had the idea that material culture shown through the language of a museum might be a good opportunity to provide access to the general public to Muslim cultures, in a way that reaches audiences that go beyond academic circles. He felt that a museum could compliment, reinforce and deepen this strategy that consists in creating better cultural contacts between the West and the Muslim world."[5] The idea of the Museum evolved over time, as did its precise location. Luis Monreal explains: "His Highness thought about several possible locations, initially in London, but gradually the idea emerged that this entity could be effective in North America. Toronto was the logical choice for a number of reasons. The first is the pluralistic environment that exists in Canada, as His Highness has often stated. It is an environment that is very open, very liberal and very curious about other cultures and civilizations, including Islam. Secondly, Toronto is strategically placed – there are sixty to seventy million people within one hour's flying distance, constituting a potentially very significant audience for the Museum. The favourable attitude of government instances and civil society to this project in Canada was another determining factor. It was also a happy coincidence that a piece of land was found next to another project that had already been started – the Ismaili Centre in Toronto, designed by Charles Correa. His Highness the Aga Khan availed himself of an opportunity to join two large sites and create an interesting landscaping project in an excellent location."[6]

A model photograph by Maki and Associates
shows the main entrance to the Museum with
the auditorium dome to the left.

An image of the Alhambra (Granada, Spain, *c.* 1350), cited by the landscape architect Vladimir Djurovic as one of the sources of his inspiration for the design of the Wynford Drive gardens.

His Highness the Aga Khan has called on the Lebanese landscape designer, Vladimir Djurovic, to create the gardens that will surround the Aga Khan Museum and the Ismaili Centre on their Wynford Drive site. With his powerful and often minimalist style, Djurovic has succeeded in unifying the work of two different architects, while distilling what might best be described as an essence of the Islamic garden and offering the public of Toronto a place of calm and inspiration. "We did not copy any garden," says Vladimir Djurovic, "it is more about what you feel and smell and hear in an Islamic garden. What it is that I love about Alhambra is the sound of water and the smell of jasmine. I wanted to use a very contemporary language."[7] This reference to a prestigious example of an Islamic garden is no coincidence. The peaceful coexistence of Muslims, Christians and Jews in the al-Andalus of history makes the Alhambra an example in more ways than one. The essence of the Islamic garden interpreted in a modern way by Vladimir Djurovic might also be seen as an extension of the pluralist credo of the Aga Khan Museum.

A rendering by Vladimir Djurovic
Landscape Architecture of the gardens shows
the glass dome of the Ismaili Centre
(architect: Charles Correa) in the background.

Referring to Maki's Delegation building in Ottawa, the Aga Khan gave some background to his goals there, and also underlined his broad commitment to future generations: "In Canada the question was what issues the members of the community felt should be addressed. There was a sense that they wanted to be seen as forward-looking, educated people who could remain true to their traditions but were not fearful of modernity or the future. They wanted, in a sense, to Islamicize modernity rather than to have modernity impact Islam. We did a survey to try to understand what the younger generations in Canada were thinking. If we were going to build a building that was going to be there for fifty years or whatever, what should that building be? They were talking about aspirations for the future; they were talking about integrating themselves with the environment in which they live, which is an environment of quality modern buildings. They were looking for modernity, but they were also looking for empathy with Islamic traditions. We have that empathy. We have not gone to an anti-cultural building, but rather a cultural building where the inspiration is modernity plus some of the value systems from the Islamic world. One of them is open space."[8]

As these computer renderings demonstrate, the landscape architect has taken into account the changing seasons in his design of the gardens that surround the Aga Khan Museum and the Ismaili Centre.

Above, **Birds on a Silk Samite Robe (detail)**
Iran, 8th–11th century; or China, 8th century (?)
Length: 124 cm
AKM 00676

Right, Prince and Princess Sadruddin Aga
Khan's "Salon Persan" in Bellerive Castle,
Geneva, Switzerland. Princess Catherine
has generously donated the showcases and
ceramics of this room to the Aga Khan Museum,
where it will be reconstituted as seen here.

The idea of openness and modernity certainly permeates the design for the new Aga Khan Museum in Toronto, an institution that will seek to branch out far beyond its own walls and also beyond the traditional concept of a museum that shows old objects in a static way. Although an emphasis will be placed on temporary exhibitions, the art works, documents, paintings and objects collected by the Aga Khan will themselves speak of modernity and openness in ways echoed by the architecture itself. They also speak of more esoteric pursuits: the late Prince Saddrudin Aga Khan, whose exquisite miniatures are now part of the Aga Kham Museum Collection, said: "Behind each illustration, there is a hidden meaning – the struggle between good and evil, the secrets of the universe, the meaning of life and death. Interpreting each picture requires considerable knowledge and concentration. If you look at it quickly you miss most of the true dimension of the picture." [9]

Above, **Honey-Coloured Glass Bottle**
Egypt or Syria, 11th–12th century
Glass, mould blown;
height 28 cm
AKM 00648

Right, **Marble Funerary Stele**
Made out of a Roman Baluster
North Africa, kufic text dated AH 377 (AD 987)
Marble; height 59.7 cm
AKM 00662

Prince Amyn Aga Khan explains the fundamental link between His Highness's goals of encouraging pluralism and the contents of a museum dedicated to Islamic art: "I think the collection shows the diversity that exists within the cultural expressions of a single religion. I believe that a number of young people will be amazed by the so-called modernity of these objects. Much of the art of Islam is not as baroque and charged and heavy as one might imagine. It is, on the contrary, very simple and very linear, and in that sense these objects tie in well with much of the Western modern aesthetic. I think that ultimately pluralism is something that attracts people. Canadians have always shown a great interest and a great willingness to learn about the Third World or the non-Anglo-Saxon world. I think that they will be naturally curious to see this collection."[10]

Far left, **Incense Burner in the Form of a Cockerel (detail)**
Iran, Khorasan, 11th century
Bronze inlaid with copper; height 28 cm
AKM 00602

Left, an interior rendering of the Aga Khan Museum by Maki and Associates intended to indicate the ambiance of the space more than the design specifics of the displays.

It is rare that the concept of a museum embraces ambitions that far surpass its own collections. In this instance there is at the heart of the project an affirmed concern for pluralism, for mutual understanding. Quality – from the objects exhibited to the architecture and landscape design – is part of a concept that implies respect for the visitor and the very generosity of spirit that is being willed forth in every visitor who is able to see and understand. The fact that the Aga Khan Museum will be alive with music, films, lectures and educational activities will serve to further emphasize the myriad creativity of Islam, and also allow those with an open eye and mind to feel the fundamental energy that expresses a religion, but also a shared humanity. Seeing the fundamental 'modernity' in an ancient ceramic or a line of calligraphy might seem to be the province of an art specialist, whereas here, in the Aga Khan Museum, this discovery, the same one that ties the present to the past and the future, is the fundamental message. It is in eliciting the "empathy with Islamic traditions" of which the Aga Khan speaks that this Museum has the possibility for making a very real contribution to respect and tolerance, but also, ultimately, to the spirit. In his letter to Fumihiko Maki, written when the Japanese architect was selected to design the Museum, His Highness the Aga Khan asked if light might not be the theme of the building: the light of God's creation, but also the light that glows from within, the light of human creativity and openness.

1 His Highness the Aga Khan, speech on the occasion of the signing of the Funding Agreement for the Global Centre for Pluralism, Ottawa, Canada, 25 October 2006. "As Canadians know so well, the idea of pluralism is not a new one in this world. It has honourable and ancient foundations, including deep roots in Islamic tradition. What is new, today, is that society is globalized, intimately interconnected and extraordinarily interdependent."
2 Speech by His Highness the Aga Khan, Toronto, Canada, 8 October 2002.
3 'Using the Former Canadian War Museum to Its Full Potential: The Global Centre for Pluralism', Global Centre for Pluralism press release, 18 October 2006.
4 Prince Amyn Aga Khan, speech at the Calouste Gulbenkian Museum, Lisbon, Portugal, 13 March 2008.
5 Interview with Luis Monreal by the author, Geneva, Switzerland, 10 June 2008.
6 Ibid.
7 Interview with Vladimir Djurovic by the author, Paris, France, 31 January 2007.
8 Interview with His Highness the Aga Khan by the author, London, United Kingdom, 6 March 2007.
9 June Ducas, "Hidden Secrets of the Universe" at: http://www.amaana.org/ISWEB/sadruddin.htm, from the *Daily Telegraph* (UK), 24 January 1998.
10 Prince Amyn Aga Khan, speech at the Calouste Gulbenkian Museum, Lisbon, Portugal, 13 March 2008.

THE AGA KHAN MUSEUM

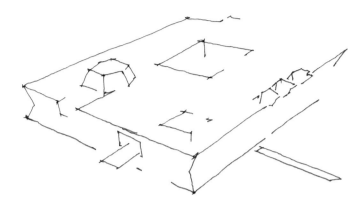

F. M.

Al-Nur (The Light): The Architecture of Fumihiko Maki

*Allah is the Light of the heavens and the earth. The Parable of
His Light is as if there were a Niche and within it a Lamp: the Lamp
enclosed in Glass: the glass as it were a brilliant star: Lit from
a blessed Tree, an Olive, neither of the east nor of the west, whose
oil is well-nigh luminous, though fire scarce touched it: Light
upon Light! Allah doth guide whom He will to His Light: Allah doth
set forth Parables for men: and Allah doth know all things.*

Qur'an, *Sura* 24:35

In a sense, the entire effort of His Highness the Aga Khan, beginning with his on-going dedication to the Ismaili community, and continuing with such exceptional initiatives as the Aga Khan Award for Architecture or the Aga Khan Program for Islamic Architecture (AKPIA) at Harvard University and the Massachusetts Institute of Technology (MIT), has been leading to this. A Museum dedicated not only to the display of exceptional objects of Islamic art, but also to music, to education – and to a sense of pluralism and openness that he found in Canada, but that he first and foremost finds in Islam. When His Highness decided that the noted Japanese architect Fumihiko Maki would design the new Museum,[1] he wrote him a long letter. In that letter the Aga Khan stated: "For the Aga Khan Museum, I thought that 'light' might be a concept around which you could design an outstanding museum. The notion of light has transversed nearly all of human history, and has been an inspiration for numerous faiths, going as far back of course to the Zoroastrians and their reverence for the Sun, to the *Sura* in the Holy Qur'an titled *al-Nur*. Decades of Western history are referred to as the 'enlightenment' for good reason."[2]

Presentations of contemporary architecture tend to focus on practical details and indeed these are important in order to understand how a building will look and how it will function. Then, too, the aesthetic notions and theories brought to bear by famous architects usually colour public perception of a building. Fumihiko Maki might best be described as modest and refined in his expression; his is not the bombastic vocabulary of those who pretend to invent whole new types of architecture. He is a

Left, a sketch by Fumihiko Maki shows the Aga Khan Museum in an 'aerial' perspective.

Above, a night rendering of the Museum shows that to a certain extent it will glow from within.

A site plan shows the Aga Khan Museum opposite the Ismail Centre as they are inserted into the Wynford Drive site.

An aerial view of the entire Wynford Drive site prior to the commencement of construction.

man of modernity who is not dismissive of the past, and these factors are important in situating the design and architecture of the future Aga Khan Museum. In many ways, the architecture is really about the uses planned for a building whose true function is not so much the display of art as it is education in the broadest sense. Beyond such practical considerations, however, the real theme of the architecture will be the ephemeral miracle of light, in the physical and artistic definitions of the word. Few, if any, symbolic starting points for a museum could be as inclusive and yet specific as the Aga Khan's reference to light. This theme justifies the conclusion that much of the activity of the Aga Khan has been leading to this Museum – in the sense that it is a distillation of everything he has expressed interest in – from architecture to the meeting of peoples and minds: a ray of light passing through a translucent wall. The message of pluralism and of the wealth of Islamic traditions that will be embodied in the Aga Khan Museum will have to encounter receptive eyes of course, but with the art selected, and the architecture designed, everything has been done to make it possible to bridge the gap between Islam and the West that the Aga Khan perceives as a central problem of the contemporary world.

This abstract, but inclusive, reference to Islam will indeed be part of the Aga Khan Museum, but it will of course be a modern, efficient building allowing for an innovative programme. As described in a report from Toronto's Commissioner for Economic Development, Culture and Tourism: "On 8 October 2002, the Aga Khan Development Network (AKDN) announced its intention to establish in Toronto a

museum housing exceptional collections of Islamic art and heritage items, as well as a cultural and educational centre devoted to the study and practice of human pluralism. The location for this proposed development is a seven-hectare site located on Wynford Drive in the north-west quadrant of the Don Valley Parkway and Eglinton Avenue. The site includes a 3.6-hectare parcel upon which the AKDN had previously proposed constructing a mosque, and an adjacent 3.35-hectare parcel that the AKDN has recently acquired from Bata Industries." In its conclusion, the report states: "The AKDN proposal would appear to be a major acquisition for the City of Toronto, and demonstrates that the world recognizes Toronto's long-standing tradition of tolerance. It further adds to Toronto's appeal as a vibrant international city

capable of competing for prominent business, research and cultural attractions. This announcement made world coverage in many major newspapers, increasing Toronto's worldwide profile."[3]

Luis Monreal, the General Manager of the Aga Khan Trust for Culture (AKTC), underlines the significance of the Museum in the present world situation: "The evolution of the political situation in the last few years, its resulting crises, and the additional factor of flows of emigration toward the West, have revealed – often dramatically – the considerable lack of knowledge of the Muslim world in Western societies. This ignorance spans all aspects of Islam: its pluralism, the diversity of the interpretations of the Qur'anic faith, the chronological and geographical extension

A computer rendering by Vladimir Djurovic Landscape Architecture shows the gardens and reflecting pools between the Aga Khan Museum by Fumihiko Maki (right) and the Ismaili Centre by Charles Correa (left).

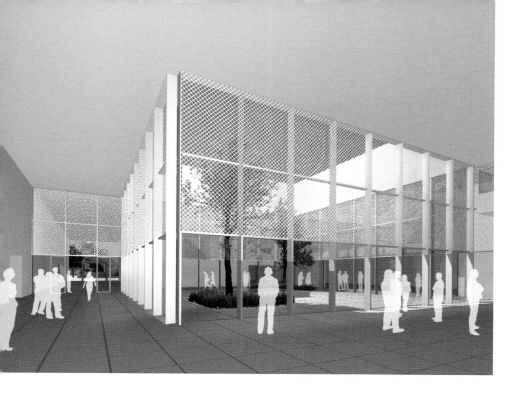

Full-height glazing reveals the inner courtyard of the Aga Khan Museum in this rendering by Maki and Associates.

of its history and culture, as well as the ethnic, linguistic and social diversity of its peoples. The supposed 'shock of civilizations' is in reality nothing more than the manifestation of the mutual ignorance that exists between two long-time neighbouring worlds. For this reason, the idea of creating a museum of Muslim culture, as an eminently educational institution with the aim of informing the North American public as to the diversity and importance of Muslim civilization, naturally imposed itself in the AKTC's programmes."[4]

The "centre devoted to the study and practice of human pluralism" referred to in the 2002 report is taking form, but in a different location. The Global Centre for Pluralism will be located in the former Canadian War Museum on Sussex Drive in Ottawa. The description of the Museum remains accurate. After the original site planning by Sasaki Associates, the architects, first Charles Correa (Ismaili Centre) and then Fumihiko Maki (Aga Khan Museum), began to work on adjacent parcels of the Wynford Drive site. The 11,000-square-metre Museum will be laid out on three floors: two floors above grade and one below for parking and reserves. The two floors above ground will contain 1800 square metres of gallery space for temporary and permanent exhibitions, a multi-purpose auditorium, a restaurant, private reception spaces, and educational areas consisting of classrooms and a library. "There is a symmetrical dome that corresponds to the auditorium: from the outside it signals the presence of the Museum, and, inside, it gives added height to the space. I am inclined to use stainless steel on the dome and canopy, but this is not yet decided,"

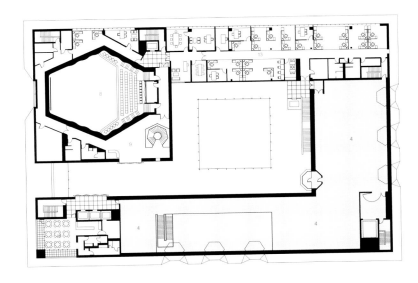

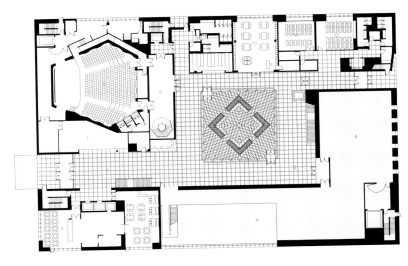

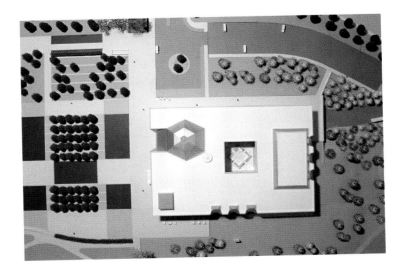

Above, the two main levels of the Aga Khan Museum are seen in these floor plans, showing the auditorium to the upper left of each drawing.

Below, an 'aerial' view of the site showing the roof of the Museum.

In this rendering, the white stone of the Museum takes on something of the colour of the daylight, as intended by the architect.

says Maki. A high room also projects above the essentially rectangular volume of the whole building, offering a special space for receptions and meetings. Though much less visible, the underground spaces will be quite ample: "We have a basement level for storage and a large parking garage below the garden. Toronto does not allow too many cars on the surface, so a great deal of parking for the Ismaili Centre and the Museum is below ground."

As for the overall character of the building, Fumihiko Maki states: "Contained within a simple rectilinear footprint, the four primary functions will revolve around a central courtyard, which will act as the heart of the building and will integrate the differing functions into a cohesive whole while allowing each space to maintain its independence, privacy and character."[5] Eighty-one metres long by fifty-four metres wide, the building is described by the architect as "compact," a fact related as much to the site and its future development as it is to the need to create a cohesive whole. "We were asked to create a museum of a certain size," says Maki, "but we decided to make it fairly compact because the possibility of future expansion was part of the programme we were given, though no precise size was determined." The expansion of the Museum is certainly not on the agenda for the moment, nor indeed is the design predetermined in any sense by the positioning issues evoked by the architect; rather, future expansion plans are permitted through the orientation of the present building and its compact form. "The placement of the Ismaili Centre," continues Maki, "and the need to create green barriers around the site to protect it from traffic noise made

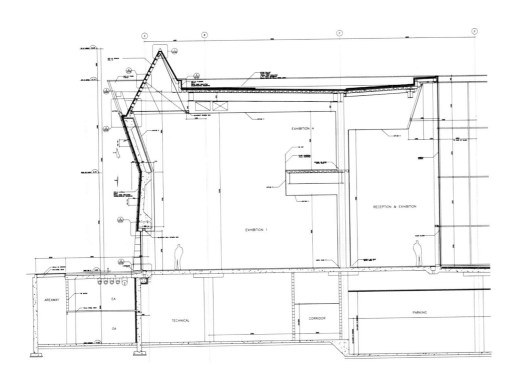

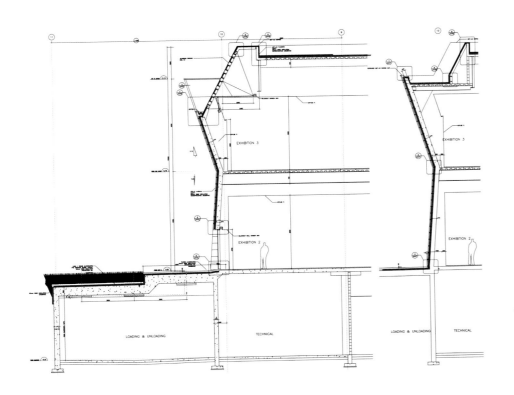

Two wall section drawings through the Museum show the angled exterior, metal skylights, interior exhibition spaces and the technical and parking areas below grade.

the precise orientation and location of the Museum fairly evident. Aside from the exhibition of art, His Highness wished to hold events such as concerts in the Museum, and there is also sizeable space for educating children about Islamic art. A shop and restaurant that can be used even by those not entering the Museum are provided for. This is not just a museum, it is actually more of a cultural centre. We felt that a compact form would allow for the required functions and good communication between them."[6]

Although the interior configuration has not yet been fully determined, Fumihiko Maki explains some of the main characteristics of the galleries: "We have tried to optimize the exhibition space to allow different configurations depending on the types of shows that might be concerned. The precise division of the spaces, essentially two L-shaped galleries – one on the ground floor and one directly above, on the first floor – is not yet determined, but there will be one area allowing for more considerable ceiling height." Maki is also allowing for the relatively small volume of the "Salon Persan", a room with Nasrid-style showcases in which Prince Sadruddin Aga Khan kept his precious collection of Islamic ceramics, in Geneva. These have been generously donated to the Museum by his widow, Princess Catherine Aga Khan. Some sculptures from Prince Sadruddin's collection will be integrated into the gardens and courtyard of the Museum. The current proposal for the courtyard, including an elaborate geometric pattern in the stonework, may in fact be the clearest reference to Islamic decorative traditions in the Museum.

Far left, **Portrait of Sultan Selim II (ruled 1566–74) (detail)**
Attributed to Haydar Reis (Nigari)
Turkey, Istanbul, c. 1570
Opaque watercolour and gold on paper;
page: 44.2 × 31.2 cm
AKM 00219

Left, **Fatimid Jar**
Egypt, 10th–11th century
Earthenware, lustre on an opaque white glaze;
height 29 cm
AKM 00548

Right, **Calligraphic Ceramic Vase**
Kufic inscription: "Blessing to its owner"
Probably Nishapur, Iran,
late 9th–early 10th century
Earthenware, white slip with black slip
decoration under a transparent glaze;
height 19.8 cm
AKM 00544

One of Fumihiko Maki's most recently completed projects, the Shimane Museum of Ancient Izumo (Taisha, Izumo City, Shimane, Japan, 2006).

Born in Tokyo in 1928, Fumihiko Maki is one of the foremost architects in the world. After receiving his Bachelor's degree in Architecture from the University of Tokyo (1952), he went on to obtain Master's degrees from both the Cranbrook Academy of Art (1953) and the Harvard Graduate School of Design (1954). This international education might be considered unusual for Japanese architects, but Maki came from a privileged background that encouraged such openness. He worked for Skidmore, Owings & Merrill in New York (1954–55) and Sert Jackson and Associates in Cambridge, Massachusetts (1955–58), before creating his own firm, Maki and Associates, in Tokyo in 1965. Maki's study and early work in the United States undoubtedly influenced him. He has always demonstrated a skilful and subtle use of modern forms and materials, while respecting elements of Japanese tradition, albeit in a contemporary way. Recent and current work by Fumihiko Maki includes the Shimane Museum of Ancient Izumo (Taisha, Izumo City, Shimane, completed in 2006), a structure similar in size to the Aga Khan Museum that uses a dynamic combination of glass and Corten steel, and the World Trade Center Tower 4 (New York), a sleek sixty-one-storey skyscraper to be completed in 2012.

Two of Fumihiko Maki's Tokyo buildings from the 1980s, Tepia (Minato-ku, Tokyo, completed in 1989), a pavilion for the display of high technology, and Spiral (Minato-ku, Tokyo, 1985), might be selected to evoke some of the qualities that His Highness the Aga Khan detected in his work. Both of these buildings place an emphasis on metal facades, but they also share a carefully studied use of light. It might be

A rendering of the World Trade Center Tower 4, designed by Maki and Associates, shows the 61-storey structure, which will be completed in 2012 (New York City, New York, USA).

noted in passing that Japanese tradition sees the light or wind that enters a building as manifestations of nature, no matter how chaotic the surrounding urban environment might be. Within Tepia and Spiral, the visitor retains a sense of calm and light, far from the dynamic life of Tokyo's streets. There is also a pronounced silence about the interiors of these buildings, even though Spiral is used for commercial activities as well as the display of art or events. Material and its manifestations, such as the perforated steel screens used in Tepia, or the floating fifteen-metre-diameter spiral ramp that gives its name to the earlier building, are one of Maki's strongest points as an architect. The quality of Japanese construction may allow for greater refinement in some instances than can be achieved outside his native country, but Maki's sense of detail, surfaces and volumes is unequalled in contemporary architecture.

Although the numerous cultural facilities that Fumihiko Maki has worked on obviously qualify him for the design of the Aga Khan Museum, it should be noted that he has almost completed another building in Canada for His Highness the Aga Khan. The Delegation of the Ismaili Imamat in Ottawa is located at 199 Sussex Drive on a one-hectare plot, neighbouring many of Canada's prominent diplomatic and political sites, such as Parliament Hill, the official residences of the Governor General and the Prime Minister, as well as numerous embassies and consulates. The building will function much like an embassy. "It will be an enabling venue for fruitful public engagements, information services and educational programmes, all backed by high-quality research, to sustain a vibrant intellectual centre and a key policy-forming

Left, a rendering by Maki and Associates of the Museum exterior emphasizes the differing colours of the facade according to its angles.

Above, His Highness the Aga Khan (left) in conversation with the architect, Fumihiko Maki.

A model photograph by Maki and Associates shows the Museum, with the emerging dome of its auditorium. The representations of the gardens are not accurate here.

institution," according to the Aga Khan. "The aim," he continues, "will be to foster policy and legislation that enables pluralism to take root in all spheres of modern life: justice, the arts, media, financial services, health and education."

To be completed in 2008, the Delegation building was the first project to be given to Fumihiko Maki by the Aga Khan. Although its nature and functions are quite different from those of the future Museum, comments made by His Highness the Aga Khan reveal some of the thinking that went into the selection of the Japanese architect: "If the mandate to the architect is to be as good as anyone in modern architecture, using modern materials and concepts but at the same time having the sensitivity to bring in external value systems, Maki was the obvious choice, because of the sensitivity of Japanese architects to their own cultural history. Linking cultural history to modernity is probably something that Japanese architects are as good at as anyone. They understand that. Maki seemed to be one to whom you could give a mandate and say, 'I am trying to bridge a number of different forces by building this modern building, and one of them is to take some of the value systems of the past, put it into this building, but not make it so esoteric that it overburdens you. It has to be inspirational and subtle.' It is not a theological building, but if, within that building, there are spaces of spirituality which we like to see as part of everyday life – it is not the exception, it should be part of everyday life –, then you are bringing that into that building. His concept of the *chahar-bagh* and the roof of the Delegation building, which plays with light and facets of glass, to me is very inspirational."[7]

An aerial perspective photograph of the model shows the Museum with its above-ground parking area and the dome of the auditorium to the left of the main entrance canopy.

The letter of His Highness the Aga Khan clearly explains the relationship of the client to the architect in this instance, expressed in terms of the ephemeral but essential qualities of light. "I hope that the building and the spaces around it will be seen as the celebration of Light, and the mysteries of Light, that nature and the human soul illustrate to us at every moment in our lives," states the Aga Khan. "I have explained at the beginning of this letter why I think Light would be an appropriate design direction for the new museum and this concept is of course particularly validated in Islamic texts and sciences: apart from the innumerable references in the Qur'an to Light in all its forms, in nature and in the human soul, the light of the skies, their sources and their meaning have for centuries been an area of intellectual inquiry and more specifically in the field of astronomy. Thus the architecture of the building would seek to express these multiple notions of Light, both natural and man-made, through the most purposeful selection of internal and external construction materials, facets of elevations playing with each other through the reflectivity of natural or electric light, and to create light gain or light retention from external natural sources or man-made internal and external sources."[8]

Quite obviously, the architect has taken the references to light by the Aga Khan to heart both in purely symbolic terms and in practical ones. The architect has been careful to create ideal conditions for the viewing of Islamic art, providing very low luminosity where the exquisite miniatures from the Aga Khan Collection might be shown, for example. Skylight screens with geometric patterns "inspired by the

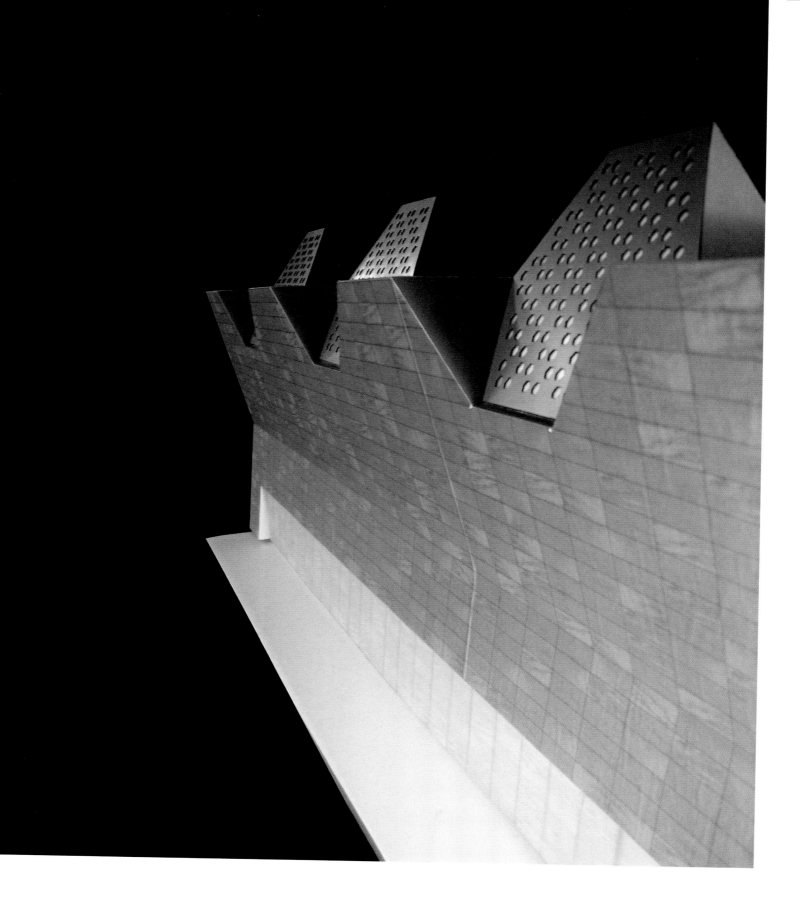

windows in mosques" and translucent marble walls will be features of the exhibition spaces. The design is centred around a courtyard, intended as "a symbolic space, protected from the outside world," with an "inherent link to traditional Islamic architecture." The exterior of the Museum is "inspired by the forms and shapes of precious stones" and will have walls inclined at two distinct angles to accentuate the play of light on the surfaces. Translucent marble and opaque white marble are likely to be the main cladding materials, although white granite was still being considered as this book went to press. As for the relation with Correa's Ismaili Centre, Fumihiko Maki states: "The metallic roof of the auditorium space will further accentuate the shape and materiality of a precious stone and is intended to establish a formal dialogue with the crystal roof of Correa's Ismaili Centre, adjacent to the Aga Khan Museum. The primary entrance and axis of the Museum is aligned with the Ismaili Centre, which will provide a subtle relationship between the two buildings, emphasizing the unity of the complex."

Though he wishes for such references to be subtle, Fumihiko Maki does reveal some of the sources of his thought where light is concerned. "The angular facade is able to refract natural light in quite an interesting way – but the final effect will only be visible when the building is completed. The cladding of the building, in white marble or white granite, will assume different colours according to the light conditions." More specifically, Maki says: "At sunset the Taj Mahal glows red or pink, while it appears to be white at noon." The use of an angled facade of this nature

Angled metal openings in the facade allow a limited amount of light into the Museum in a style that brings to mind a sublimated reference to the Shaykh Lutfallah Mosque (Isfahan, Iran, 1603–19).

In this rendering by Maki and Associates of the exterior of the Aga Khan Museum the white simplicity of the design is emphasized, with different colours and shading visible on the facade according to the time of day and the angle of the sun.

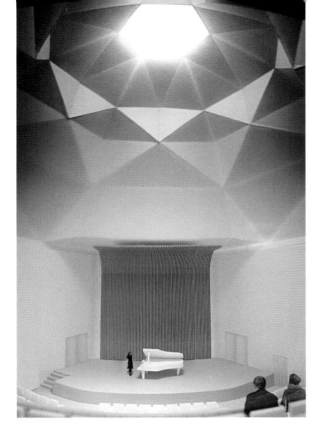

has never been attempted by Maki, but full-scale mock-ups have been erected near the site to confirm the effects of light, or indeed those of climate, on the planned stone cladding. The architect goes on to refer to the interior of the Museum, stating: "There is some natural light but we tried to make the openings very carefully since much of the material exhibited is very sensitive to light. I feel that references to Islamic architecture should be abstract in this instance, and the screens we have developed respond to this approach. The choice of cladding materials – white marble or white granite – will allow for a certain translucency from the inside, perhaps a bit like the marble used in the Beinecke Rare Book Library at Yale designed by Gordon Bunshaft [Skidmore, Owings & Merrill, New Haven, Connecticut, 1963]."[9] In explaining the interior forms of the dome that tops the Museum's auditorium, Maki makes specific reference to a dome: "The stage of the auditorium recalls the domes of Islam – perhaps the Bazaar in Kashan, Iran, for example." The angled skylights introduced into the museum design by the architect are of course abstract, but his own documentation refers to the very subtle windows of the Shaykh Lutfallah Mosque (Isfahan, Iran, 1603–19).

It would appear that the references of Fumihiko Maki, ranging from ancient Iran and the Taj Mahal in India to a work by Gordon Bunshaft, correspond quite directly to the Aga Khan's words concerning the Ottawa Delegation building: "If the

Left, light cascades through a skylight in a dome of the Bazaar in Kashan, Iran.

Above, the interior of the dome of the auditorium of the Aga Khan Museum draws some of its inspiration from such references.

A sunset view of the dome of the Taj Mahal, in Agra, the last and greatest architectural and artistic achievement of the Mughal period, erected on the orders of Shah Jahan (1592–1658). Fumihiko Maki cites the changing colours of the stone of the Taj Mahal as a reference to the effect he is seeking in Toronto.

mandate to the architect is to be as good as anyone in modern architecture, using modern materials and concepts but at the same time having the sensitivity to bring in external value systems, Maki was the obvious choice." Fumihiko Maki concludes: "His Highness didn't want this particular building to use overtly Islamic forms or references. He wanted to have a modern building appropriate to its context." In what may be his most significant remark about the building, Fumihiko Maki says, "we want to have quiet spaces." Situated in a rather busy area of Toronto, the Aga Khan Museum will be surrounded by gardens designed by Vladimir Djurovic, and its powerful walls speak of a sense of protection, of a place to leave the everyday world behind and to plunge into the wonders of civilizations that may not be familiar for many visitors.

It is important however to underline the fact that Islam and, indeed, spirituality are a constant factor in the activities of the Aga Khan, and that such a presence may not only make itself felt through specific citations, albeit abstract ones, of Islamic architecture. Nor would it be appropriate to exclusively analyze the work of Maki in this instance as a piece of contemporary architecture. The Aga Khan Museum will indeed be a modern facility and through its many planned activities, its education,

Muqarnas on the Shaykh Lutfallah Mosque built by Shah Abbas I in Isfahan, Iran, from 1603–19. Fumihiko Maki cites this structure as an influence on his design for the Aga Khan Museum.

music and performance programmes, it will reach out and plead for the pluralism that is at the heart of the message conveyed by the Aga Khan himself.

The dedication of the Aga Khan to architecture, seen in such ongoing programmes as the Aga Khan Award for Architecture, has to do more with improving the conditions of life of a vast part of humanity than it does with heralding a new architectural style. Pointedly, the Aga Khan refers to architecture as part of "the processes of change" – a terminology that may be at odds with most descriptions of contemporary buildings. When asked if, for him, building is not in fact a way of bringing people together, he responds: "Yes, or giving them a sense of individuality. Sometimes they need that also. I think spirituality is not necessarily experienced only in a societal context, it can be very much an individual thing. There are certain times when you need to create space where spirituality can be experienced individually. I think of parks as places where the individual is very powerful. We have also worked recently on dormitories for universities. What the West would think of as secular spaces, in our context very often are not exclusively secular. They actually seek to have a content in an area or in the totality of the building which has an additional

message or an additional sense to it. In the Islamic world we always look at the fundamental unity of *dîn* and *dunya*, of spirit and life, and we cannot tolerate that one functions without the other. The notion of *dîn* and *dunya* and the integrity of human life is a very important issue." [10]

It is surely in the "quiet spaces" of the Aga Khan Museum that the talent of Fumihiko Maki will be felt, and the connection between the client and the architect will be most readily apparent. The Museum will be a vibrant place, full of life and art, but it will also be a quiet one, where the sense of spirituality referred to by the Aga Khan will be felt by those who understand it. It is no accident that in describing "light" in his original letter to Fumihiko Maki, the Aga Khan passes directly from an evocation of a *Sura* of the Qur'an to a reference to the European Enlightenment. The light he refers to crosses through civilizations and religions – it is the source of life and art, the two forces being brought together in the walls of the Aga Khan Museum. The ultimate message of pluralism and tolerance conveyed by His Highness the Aga Khan might best be summed up in this instance by his own references to the two sources of light, "natural light emanating from God's creation," and "light ... which emanates from human sources, in the form of art, culture and well-inspired human knowledge." [11]

Two renderings by Maki and Associates of the interior of the auditorium of the Aga Khan Museum.

1 Design Architects: Fumihiko Maki and Maki and Associates, Tokyo, Japan. Architect of Record: Moriyama & Teshima Architects, Toronto, Canada.
2 Letter from His Highness the Aga Khan to Fumihiko Maki, 3 January 2006.
3 Staff Report from Joe Halstead, Commissioner Economic Development, Culture and Tourism to the Economic Development and Parks Committee of the City of Toronto, 20 November 2002.
4 Luis Monreal, *Splendori a Corte: Un'anteprima del Museo Aga Khan di Toronto*, Milan, Italy, 2007.
5 Fumihiko Maki and Maki and Associates, <Aga Khan Museum 007. 02. 17.pdf>. Document provided by the architects to the author.
6 Interview with Fumihiko Maki by the author, Basel, Switzerland, 13 May 2008.
7 Interview with His Highness the Aga Khan by the author, London, United Kingdom, 6 March 2007.
8 Letter from His Highness the Aga Khan to Fumihiko Maki, 3 January 2006.
9 Interview with Fumihiko Maki by the author, Basel, Switzerland, 13 May 2008.
10 Interview with His Highness the Aga Khan by the author, London, United Kingdom, 6 March 2007.
11 Letter from His Highness the Aga Khan to Fumihiko Maki, 3 January 2006.

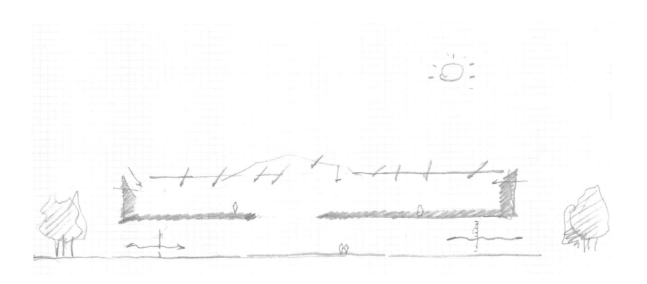

What the Aga Khan Museum Will Seek to Accomplish

*One of the central elements of the Islamic faith is
the inseparable nature of faith and world. The two are so deeply
intertwined that one cannot imagine their separation.
They constitute 'a way of life'.*

His Highness the Aga Khan

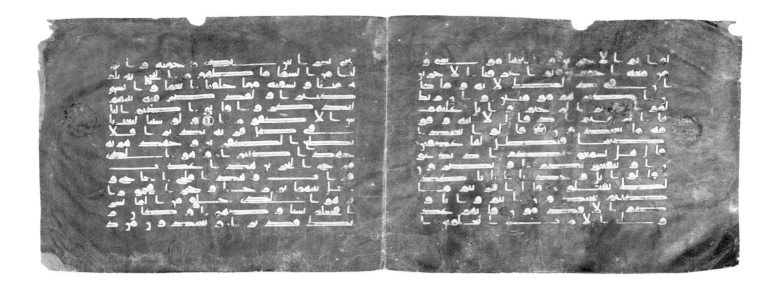

The Aga Khan Museum has been defined from the outset as a haven for varied activities – going far beyond the more traditional role of a museum as a place to exhibit works of art. Given its pluralist ambitions and the very diversity of Islamic art, the institution is logically organized to offer educational opportunities, concerts, lectures, films and, in a less public mode, conservation of the artworks. These goals correspond clearly to the emphasis placed by His Highness the Aga Khan on education initiatives and on the effort to familiarize the West with the cultural traditions of Islam. The Aga Khan Museum will also organize temporary exhibitions that will range in theme from periods or dynasties of Islamic civilization to thematic and historic presentations.

Prince Amyn Aga Khan underlines some of the real goals of this varied programme: "I would hope that we will have seminars and discussion groups, and that we will even have certain types of classes, and that we will do research work too. I hope that the initial feeling will be one of surprise and amazement. That's what a museum should do for you – give you the feeling that you have discovered something that you hadn't suspected had existed beforehand. After surprise and amazement, I hope it will be admiration. After admiration, ideally, it will be understanding. I should like to think that the Aga Khan Museum will help visitors to look on other human beings in other parts of the world with more comprehension. Ideally, a museum should allow those who view its collections to increase their knowledge. Every increase in knowledge increases one's understanding."[1]

Left, a sketch by Fumihiko Maki of a section of the Aga Khan Museum.

Above, **Qur'an Folio in Gold Kufic Script on Blue Parchment**
North Africa, 9th–10th century
Ink, gold, and silver (now oxidized)
on blue-dyed parchment;
28.6 × 35 cm
AKM 00477

Above, an exhibition entitled
The Path of Princes: Masterpieces of Islamic Art from the Aga Khan Museum Collection,
at the Calouste Gulbenkian Foundation, Lisbon, Portugal, in 2008.

Right, **Standard (*alam*) (detail)**
Iran, 16th century
Steel; 103 × 32 cm
AKM 00615

Luis Monreal, the General Manager of the Aga Khan Trust for Culture (AKTC), explains: "The Toronto Museum is original in several respects. The first is its ambition to be an active educational institution, having the target to reach audiences in both the United States and Canada. It will have a limited, but distinguished, permanent collection and a large space and programme for temporary exhibitions. The themes of these shows will be related to the Muslim world and conceived to attract large numbers of people. There will be three or four temporary exhibitions a year. These shows may deal with major moments or dynasties of Islam, or in other cases with more imaginative subjects like the relationship of Muslim cultures and China through the Silk Route. Science in the Muslim world might be another subject, or the relationship between calligraphy and other art forms, for example."[2]

The organization of exhibitions and the relationship of the Aga Khan Museum with other institutions that collect Islamic art are indeed a centrepiece of its overall strategy. Luis Monreal continues: "These exhibitions will use objects lent by public institutions or private collectors and the effort to stage the shows will be shared with other museums in Europe and North America in an informal ad hoc federation of interests. The masterpieces of Islamic art exhibitions which previewed the Aga Khan Museum Collections in Parma [Italy], London, Paris, Lisbon and Toledo [Spain] may give an idea of some of the institutions that will participate in these efforts. The travelling exhibition created some institutional links that will be positive for the future of the Aga Khan Museum." Nor will the activities of the Aga Khan Museum in

**The Court of Fath 'Ali Shah
(ruled 1798–1834) with Foreign
Ambassadors and Envoys (detail)**
Tehran, Iran, c. 1815
Opaque watercolour and gold on paper
32 × 125.5 cm
AKM 00502

**Engraved Brass Boat-Shaped *Kashkul*
(detail)**
Iran, second half of the 16th century
Brass; length 61 cm
AKM 00612

the area of art exhibitions be limited to pieces from much earlier times. "There may be contemporary art from the Muslim world as well. The Museum's role will also be to place contemporary art produced by Muslim artists in the spotlight," affirms Monreal.[3] It is clear that the creation of the Aga Khan Museum and its willingness to participate in the organization of travelling exhibitions will serve in some instances as a catalyst, permitting other institutions to get involved in shows that they might otherwise have considered too 'risky' vis-à-vis the investment required.

It should be emphasized that the Aga Khan Museum will take its place within a web of sister organizations, some of which are directly related to the Aga Khan Development Network (AKDN) and some of which are under university control, for example. This is the case of the Aga Khan Program for Islamic Architecture (AKPIA) at Harvard University and the Massachusetts Institute of Technology (MIT), which is dedicated to the study of Islamic architecture, visual culture and conservation in an effort to respond to the cultural and educational needs of a diverse constituency

Cast Brass Torch Stand with Chevrons (detail)
Iran, late 16th century
43.2 cm
AKM 00614

drawn from all over the world. AKPIA may well interact with the Museum according to circumstances, perhaps encouraging students to take internships in Toronto in such fields as conservation or for specific exhibitions. The Program's professors and doctoral candidates would also have access to original source materials for research purposes.

The conservation laboratory of the Museum will, of course, have its own collection as a base, but may well assist other museums in the Muslim world in the future. The launch of two other AKTC museum projects – the Museum of Historic Cairo in Azhar Park, which will be under the control of the Egyptian Supreme Council of Antiquities and with which the Aga Khan Museum will certainly have ongoing relationships, and the Indian Ocean Maritime Museum in Zanzibar – may also provide occasions for interactions or loans in the future. Geographically closer, the Global Centre for Pluralism in Ottawa will surely have a great deal in common with the goals and aspirations of the Aga Khan Museum.

Above, a rendering by Maki and Associates of low-light interior galleries intended to give an idea of the potential ambiance of the Museum rather than its design specifics.

Right, **Rustam Pursues the *Div* Akvan Disguised as an Onager (detail)**
Miniature painting attributed to Muzaffar 'Ali
Detached folio from the *Shahnameh*
of Shah Tamasp (ruled 1524–76)
Iran, Tabriz, *c.* 1530–35
Opaque watercolour, gold and ink on paper;
47 × 31.8 cm
AKM 00162

With a web of relations extending from the Louvre in Paris to the Calouste Gulbenkian Foundation in Lisbon, and far beyond through the various organizations of the Aga Khan Development Network, the Aga Khan Museum will not find itself in the position of some fledgling institutions that are obliged to make their reputation slowly over time. This Museum will emerge at the highest levels of the study, exhibition and education concerning the cultures of Islam. This substantial advantage, obviously permitted by the long-sustained efforts of His Highness the Aga Khan to promote understanding between Islam and the West, will assure that only the highest level of discussion, exhibition and cultural performance will occur under the aegis of the Museum. What Toronto receives with the Aga Khan Museum is, of course, a new institution based within its boundaries, but it is also in a very real sense an open door to other parts of the world.

A rendering of the interior of the auditorium space in the Aga Khan Museum.

Though the Aga Khan Museum will obviously have a base in material culture, its ambitions very definitely extend to non-material culture as it might be presented in the institution's state-of-the-art auditorium, for example. "The auditorium will be a platform for the Aga Khan Music Initiative in Central Asia or related efforts such as Yo Yo Ma's Silk Road project," according to Luis Monreal. The Music Initiative has undertaken a long-term collaboration with the Center for Folklife and Cultural Heritage of the Smithsonian Institution, the national museum and research complex of the United States, to create a ten-volume anthology of Central Asian music, underlining the wealth of potential activity in the area of music in Toronto. Other expressions of the music of Islam will, of course, also make their appearance in the auditorium according to programming yet to be announced. So, too, lectures, sometimes in connection with other Aga Khan programmes, and film presentations will assure that the auditorium will have a rich and continuous series of events to offer the Toronto public. Luis Monreal points out that the significant programmes of the Aga Khan Museum will include educational activities planned around the temporary exhibitions for all groups: courses in Islamic art and culture for children and adults; a music education and discovery programme; seminars and conferences appealing to scholars and researchers; a resource centre and library; as well as workshops on the visual and performing arts.

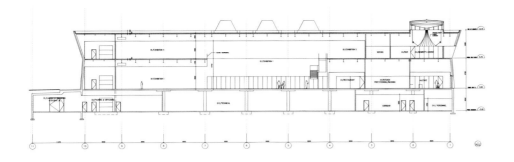

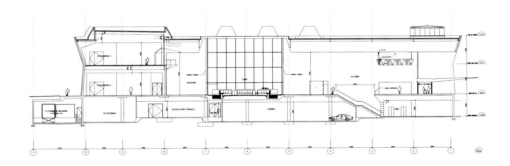

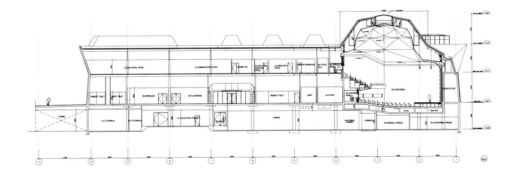

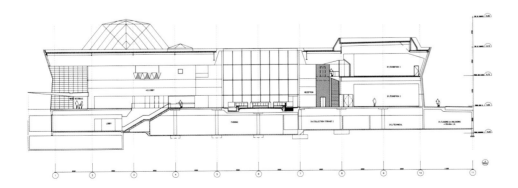

East-West section drawings cut through
various points in the Museum.

A rendering shows the interior space of the
Museum, near the floor-to-ceiling glazing of
the interior courtyard.

Museums conceived in a more traditional vein tend, of course, to place an emphasis on conservation with all its ramifications. Even the display of artwork for the public is seen by some old-school curators as a distraction from their principal task, which consists in 'conserving' or keeping a work of art in pristine condition for future generations. Scholars are indeed formed to focus on single-minded goals in many cases, which is what makes for their professional competence. The Aga Khan Museum starts from a different premise, an imperative mission of education and outreach that has to do as much with the future as it does with the past. Surely not a place of religion per se, it is nonetheless one where certain ideas have their significance. His Highness explains: "One of the central elements of the Islamic faith is the inseparable nature of faith and world. The two are so deeply intertwined that one cannot imagine their separation. They constitute 'a way of life'." [4]

Conceived as a vibrant and active institution that will mirror the diversity and complexity of Islamic culture in a broad way, the Aga Khan Museum might be seen as an important piece in a large puzzle that His Highness the Aga Khan has been patiently assembling since his accession to the Imamat in 1957. His are not necessarily initiatives that will change the world from one day to the next, rather they are based in a long-term and complex strategy that aims to reach into all levels of education and information where relations between the West and Islam are concerned. The Museum in many respects is aimed at a broader public than his universities or initiatives like the Aga Khan Award for Architecture that essentially

A low-light rendering of exhibition spaces with some natural light admitted from the sky through metal skylights seen to the right.

reach out to scholars and professionals, and yet the long-term approach of both is evident. Where knowledge of the objects or the cultures concerned lacks, there will be ways to learn within the walls of the Museum, but there will also be a place for those who are willing to be 'amazed', as Prince Amyn has stated.

One of the current Aga Khan Professors at Harvard University, Gülru Necipoglu, affirms that the AKPIA program at Harvard and MIT has had a substantial impact on Islamic studies in the United States. Her remarks have a direct bearing on the profound nature of the ambitions of the Aga Khan Museum in Toronto, even though AKPIA and the Museum are institutionally quite separate. Of the Aga Khan, she says: "He is of course interested in architecture, but I believe he imagined it, in the context of the Aga Khan Program for Islamic Architecture, as a kind of mediation between the two worlds, which are not two opposite civilizations. He emphasized the living aspect of the culture instead of burying it in the medieval past. By funding these programs, he has opened up the field. It used to be confined and esoteric. He emphasized the diversity, I think because of his own Ismaili faith – showing that there is not only one Islam. Until the 1970s there was a stereotyped vision of Islamic unity. It was viewed as being static. The emphasis on diversity made it a more real, connected study. The emphasis has gone from unity to diversity."[5]

The very concept of the Aga Khan Museum, including its architecture and landscape design, participates in its ambitions – to create a living link not only between past and present, Islam and the West, but perhaps most importantly between people,

The use of the screen-like effect seen in the image above showing the inner courtyard may recall Maki's own Japanese heritage, albeit in a very indirect and modern way.

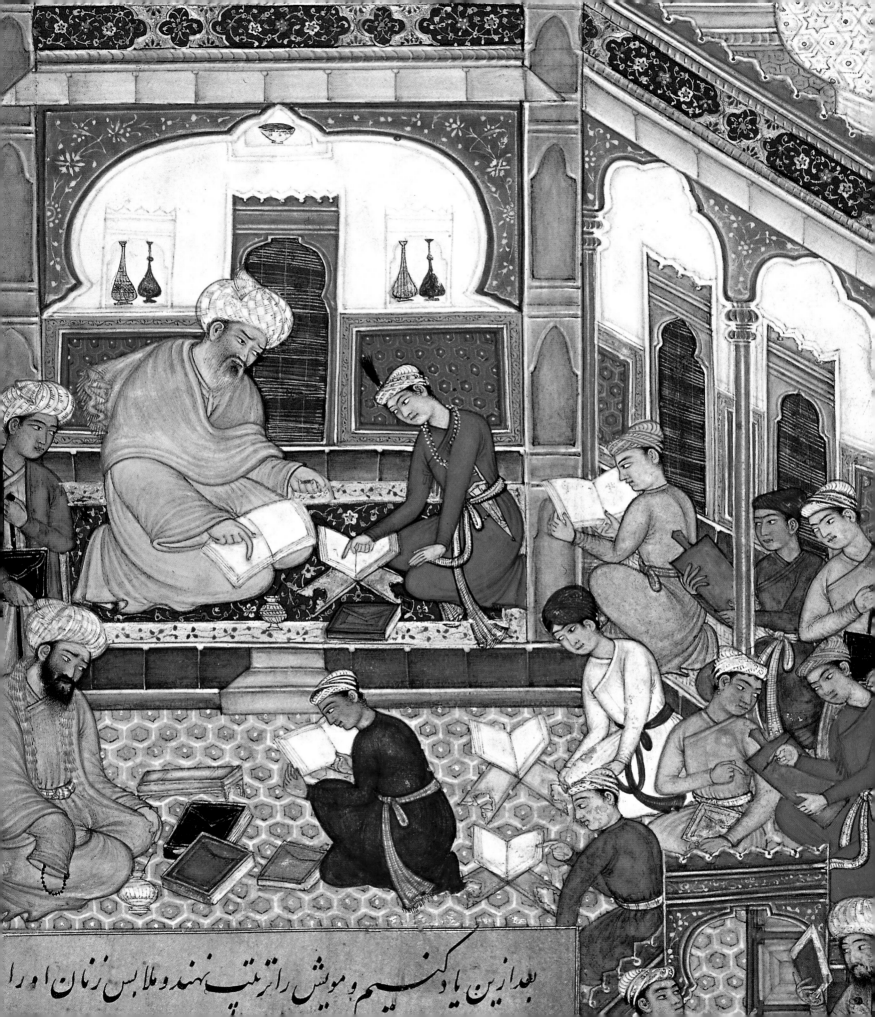

بعد ازین یادکنیم و مویش را ز تت نهند و ملابس زنان او را

who, as Prince Amyn Aga Khan says, may well be able to understand each other better if they take the time to absorb and understand some of the profound lessons embodied within its white walls.

The architect Fumihiko Maki points out that modernity was a more clearly stated goal of His Highness the Aga Khan for the new Museum than specific references to Islam. The references to Islam that exist in the architecture or the gardens are instead sublimated and rendered in their essence. Where some, in North America in particular, might well have a view of Islam as a dusty, dangerous place, here a splendid modern building, beautiful gardens and objects that tell the stories of more than a thousand and one nights open vistas to other worlds. The door that His Highness the Aga Khan opens with the new Museum is one that permits visitors to travel through time and space, but above all to look with a sense of wonder on not one but many civilizations, all based in a single religion. The very quality of the architecture of Maki, the gardens of Djurovic or such marvellous works of art as a celebrated folio from the *Shahnameh* of Shah Tamasp (ruled 1524–76) reveal the remarkable generosity of this gift to the people of Toronto and the region. If it is possible to sublimate a part of the essence of Islam in an idea such as light, the same light that touches every person, this is the place where that will happen and where open minds will meet.

1   Prince Amyn Aga Khan, speech at the Calouste
    Gulbenkian Museum, Lisbon, Portugal,
    13 March 2008.
2   Interview with Luis Monreal by the author,
    Geneva, Switzerland, 10 June 2008.
3   Ibid.
4   His Highness the Aga Khan, speech at the
    Tutzing Evangelical Academy in Tutzing, Germany,
    20 May 2006.
5   Interview with Professor Gülru Necipoglu by
    the author, Harvard University, Cambridge,
    Massachusetts, 2 November 2006.

A Garden in Toronto:
The Design of Vladimir Djurovic

*Unto those who do right shall be given an excellent reward
in this world; but the dwelling of the next life shall be better;
and happy shall be the dwelling of the pious! Namely, gardens of
eternal abode, into which they shall enter; rivers shall flow
beneath the same; therein shall they enjoy whatever they wish.
Thus will God recompense the pious.*

Qur'an, *Sura* 16:30–31

An international competition was held to select the landscape architect who would be given the task of uniting the Aga Khan Museum designed by Fumihiko Maki and the Ismaili Centre designed by Charles Correa on the seven-hectare site selected in Toronto for both institutions. The young Lebanese architect Vladimir Djurovic was chosen over far better known figures. Djurovic, a cosmopolitan figure who owes his name to his Serbian father, states the goals of his scheme in direct terms: "The competition covered the entire Wynford Drive site, and was an ideal exploration platform in search of the most appropriate solutions that could address the complex challenges of the site and the brief. In the midst of highly charged surroundings, we sought to unify and integrate the architectural volumes and provide open, welcoming spaces for all, while maintaining privacy. We also sought to create a platform for education that inspires and unifies without alienating or segregating, and a serene environment where contemplation finds spirituality."[1]

Though he is clearly inspired by modern landscape design as much as by the past, Vladimir Djurovic continues: "Our vision for the project is one that captures the essence of the Islamic garden and translates it into an expression that reflects its context and contemporary age. Embracing the five senses as the means to reach the soul, every space and every garden are imbued with the delicate sensations that we seem to have lost in this fast-paced era. The ephemeral and the eternal are both essential to our composition of spaces. Shadows, light, petals, leaves and water in motion are complemented by the solidity and purity of created forms. All is not

Left, a sketch by Vladimir Djurovic for the gardens near the Museum, showing the Ismaili Centre in the background.

Above, the sound of water accompanies the other sounds and smells of the gardens in an almost tangible way in this image.

An almost minimalist pattern of reflecting pools and trees will separate the Ismaili Centre, seen to the rear of this rendering, and the Aga Khan Museum.

Birch trees surrounded by a broken stone circle that appears to be inspired by the work of the sculptor Richard Long mark one area in the gardens surrounding the Museum.

at once apparent; the garden reveals itself slowly to the visitor, who experiences hidden aspects with serendipity." Being the designer who has to navigate the space between two such well-known architects as Maki and Correa cannot be simple, but Djurovic has succeeded in creating "a unique, harmonious and welcoming garden with two landmark buildings in it. The garden," he says, "could be viewed as fluctuating between formal spaces around the buildings and informal spaces as one moves away." Djurovic continues: "One of the main roles of the landscape scheme was to merge and compliment the architectural direction set forth by the two buildings. Their programme, interior spaces and architectural spirit had to be seamlessly extended into the outdoors, while striving to come up with one unified environment for the enjoyment of the public. The reading of two structures embedded in a memorable

park was always a main aspiration of His Highness the Aga Khan for this project. The Museum's architecture, and its evolution since inception, has been a major source of inspiration for our gardens. Its resounding presence, yet simplicity and delicacy, had to be reflected and complemented in our outdoor spaces. The surrounding gardens nestle the Museum into its site, and further amplify its experience through its arrival sequence and formal layout."[2]

Vladimir Djurovic was born to a Serbian father and a Lebanese mother in 1967. He received a degree in Horticulture from Reading University in England in 1989 and his Master's degree in Landscape Architecture from the University of Georgia in 1992, after having worked with the large landscape firm EDAW in Atlanta. Vladimir Djurovic Landscape Architecture (VDLA) was created in 1995 in Beirut, and has practiced an

The 'simplicity' expressed in the work of Vladimir Djurovic in Toronto can also be seen here in another of his projects, the Bassil Mountain Escape (Faqra, Lebanon).

Humayun's Tomb and Gardens (Delhi, India), restored in 2003 by the Aga Khan Historic Cities Programme, is cited by Vladimir Djurovic as a source of inspiration for his work in Toronto, as is the Taj Mahal (right).

intriguing mixture of minimalist architecture and landscape design since then, in particular for numerous private clients. Djurovic admits to being attracted to the craftsmanship of the Swiss architect Peter Zumthor, or to the ways in which the Portuguese architect Eduardo Souto de Moura integrates his work into its natural settings. His Samir Kassir Square (Beirut, Lebanon, 2004) was a winner of a 2007 Aga Khan Award for Architecture. Located in the recently reconstructed Beirut Central District, the 815-square-metre park was conceived around two existing ficus trees that had somehow managed to survive the violence that wracked Beirut for years. "The challenge of this project," says Djurovic, "was to create a quiet refuge on a limited piece of land surrounded by buildings, while addressing the prominent street frontage that it occupies. In essence, to become a small escape dedicated to the city and its people." A raised 'water mirror' is a central feature of the Square, faced by a twenty-metre-long solid stone bench. The jury citation for the 2007 Award reads: "The Samir Kassir Square is a restrained and serene urban public space that skilfully handles the conditions and infrastructure of its location in a city that has undergone rapid redevelopment. The Award will go to Vladimir Djurovic, the pre-eminent landscape architect working in Lebanon today."

"After I won the competition for the garden in Toronto," explains Djurovic, "His Highness gave me a list of places to visit around the world. 'Once you have visited these places, let us meet again,' he said. I had never been to India and I found the gardens of Humayun's Tomb and Fatehpur Sikri remarkable."[3]

Built in honour of Sufi saint Salim Chishti in 1571 by the Mughal emperor Akbar, Fatehpur Sikri might be considered a revealing choice in the context of the itinerary of Djurovic. Unlike other Mughal cities, it demonstrates a certain informality and improvisation, and blends influences from Hindu and Jain sources as well as Islamic elements. Further, Fatehpur Sikri is known to have influenced such modern figures as Charles and Ray Eames, and Balkrishna Doshi. After visiting India, Djurovic finished his whirlwind tour in Azhar Park in Cairo. "I realized after these visits," says the landscape architect, "that what the Aga Khan is doing is not for now, it is for generations to come. I understood that anything I do for him has to last as long as possible."

The tomb of the second Mughal emperor Humayun, who ruled modern Afghanistan, Pakistan, and parts of northern India from 1530–40 and again from 1555–56, is one of the twenty-three World Heritage Sites in India. The *chahar-bagh*, or four-part paradise garden, is the earliest existing example of the Mughal garden tomb. Humayun's Tomb and Gardens in Delhi are considered one of the precursors of the Taj Mahal. The first privately funded restoration of a World Heritage Site in India was completed in March 2003 through the joint efforts of the Aga Khan Trust for Culture (AKTC) and the Archaeological Survey of India (ASI), under the aegis of the National Culture Fund. The objective of the project was to revitalize the gardens, pathways, fountains and water channels of the garden surrounding Humayun's Tomb, according to the original plans. Valdimir Djurovic's reference to these gardens as one of his sources of inspiration for the Wynford Drive site is also revealing in that they

A rendering of the gardens shows the planting and reflecting pools next to the Ismaili Centre by Charles Correa.

Vladimir Djurovic speaks of the inspiration of Islamic gardens – such as those of the Alhambra in Granada, Spain – more in terms of sound and smell than in terms of design specifics.

are striking above all for their simplicity – a kind of minimalism 450 years before the landscape architect began to practice his own modern art.

Nor are the thoughts of the Aga Khan far from Djurovic's interest in the gardens of Humayun's Tomb, or its better known successor, the Taj Majal. The Aga Khan states: "You cannot go to a place like the Taj Mahal without being acutely aware of the site use and that is true of most of these great historic buildings. The use of gardens and water is a very strong part of Islam, that is, the references in the theological context to the quality of the environment."[4] The landscape architect's concern for the inclusiveness of the gardens in Toronto can also be related to the

Aga Khan's often repeated commitment to pluralism within a generous and open interpretation of Islam.

    The designs of Vladimir Djurovic for the 75,000-square-metre Toronto gardens are an intentional attempt to render contemporary the very spirit of the Islamic garden. "I think that His Highness is happiest when he is working and discussing the gardens. He really wants us to reinterpret the Islamic garden in a contemporary way. We did not copy any garden – it is more about what you feel and smell and hear in an Islamic garden. What it is that I love about Alhambra is the sound of water and the smell of jasmine. I wanted to use a very contemporary language. The architecture of the

A computer perspective gives a seductive idea of the future gardens of the Wynford Drive site, at once modern and yet still respectful of Islamic traditions.

The combination of water, the reflection of the sky and the flowering trees, gives this view a particularly poetic or 'otherwordly' feeling, as though a small part of the garden of paradise had found its way to Toronto.

buildings is very contemporary. The garden must reflect its context as well – a place covered with snow. I like this challenge: how to reinterpret the Islamic garden."[5]

Indeed, for an architect who has worked more in Lebanon and the Middle East than in North America, the climate of Toronto posed new challenges. "Our intent is always to produce lasting environments," he says, "both physical and aesthetic. Hence durability was a major parameter for us to focus on in this new climate, starting from choice of materials, thicknesses, details and construction techniques, as well as the appropriate selection of plant species. Our close collaboration with Moriyama & Teshima,[6] with their extensive experience in such climates and major involvement with the project, was more than instrumental in guiding, fine-tuning and resolving all the technical issues for the project to achieve its ultimate goals."[7]

After initially proposing a number of garden features near the Museum, Vladimir Djurovic opted for a simpler design in the course of numerous meetings with His Highness the Aga Khan. He states: "All the features around the Museum have been omitted now, and are articulated as a white birch *(betula alba)* forest, which embraces the entire Museum structure. There are no elements that will now disturb a serene

reading of the building embedded in a white birch grove. This will allow the sculptural qualities of the architecture to blend with nature." [8] One area of particular attention and concern in the frigid winter climate of Toronto was the use of water in the gardens. "In one preliminary scheme we created translucent cast acrylic elements with water flowing over the edges. Covered with snow, they would appear like lit ice cubes. The edges would have been angled out so that freezing ice would fall off the edge of the basins," explains the designer. This idea was abandoned in favour of solid granite basin walls because Djurovic could not vouch for the long-term reliability of acrylic slabs, which tend to turn yellow with time. Within the newly designed granite basins, their edges still angled out to allow expanding ice to fall over the edges, Djurovic places what he calls "steel lilies" that create turbulence in the water when it is liquid, and are heated in winter to produce steam and the continuing sound of water in movement. The waterfall *bustan* (Arabic for 'fruit garden'), a secluded yet welcoming space, is a niche in the botanical garden that serves as a gateway to the Ismaili Centre. A rose garden elsewhere uses the scents and origins of the varieties selected to give a subtle lesson to visitors about the geographic dispersion across the world of the Ismaili community.

Low-lying divisions structure a part of the garden where calm is the hallmark of spaces intended to give visitors a chance to contemplate what they have seen within the Museum.

Right, a closer view of the reflecting pools with the Ismaili Centre in the background.

All of the elements imagined by Vladimir Djurovic for the Wynford Drive site share a simplicity and regularity bordering on minimalism, though there are frequent surprises and changes of mood, progressing from a more formal configuration near the buildings and becoming less apparently ordered further from the heart of the site. "The park is first and foremost a giant buffer zone protecting the sanctum of the project and creating a setting for the architectural volume. It also acts as a generous gesture to the city from the Ismaili community to the people who embraced them, providing a green public environment and linking two previously disconnected parts of the city. The park is a sanctuary for wildlife and a place for people to immerse themselves in a natural environment. All plants have been selected to entice an array of birds and butterflies and a pond created to help them breed and flourish."[9] It is this essential modesty, expressed by a younger creator in the context of work with two very accomplished architects, that has allowed Vladimir Djurovic to conceive of a garden that responds to numerous requirements while retaining its own identity. Through his seductive but quite realistic computer perspectives – a number of which are published here – Djurovic has conquered the enthusiasm of those involved in the Toronto projects, giving a sense of unity to what could have become a disparate whole, especially given the decidedly urban context of the site, with major traffic arteries located just beyond this green vision of paradise. Through sight, but also sound and smell, this Lebanese designer with a Serbian name recreates an Islamic garden in a land of snow, a garden of pluralism.

Above, a very realistic computer perspective of the gardens shows that the designer has become even more minimalistic in the course of the design process, leaving only alleys and walkways through the greenery for visitors.

Right, an exterior rendering of the Museum shows the paving pattern and a reflecting pool designed by Vladimir Djurovic, and presents the white stone cladding with an orange glow.

Though the avowed and assumed modernity of the designs of the entire Wynford Drive site place it very firmly in the present, there is a deep current that runs below the gardens of Vladimir Djurovic, and that is the current of belief. It is clear that His Highness the Aga Khan has followed the work of the landscape architect with particular attention. Djurovic states: "His Highness's passion for gardens is intoxicating. His ideas for creating appropriate and memorable outdoor spaces became our main source of inspiration and motivation to truly excel in this project. His insights, recommendations and unwavering involvement throughout the design process has shaped and effectively resulted in the gardens that we have developed for this project."[10] His Highness the Aga Khan has long been interested in landscape design, and as he makes clear there are good reasons for this: "One of the issues in the Islamic world is the relationship between an ability to create and what we see of that creation. Nature is one of the evidences of God's creation. I am very sensitive to that personally."[11] In the case of the Aga Khan Museum, he wrote to Fumihiko Maki about two kinds of light – the light of God's creation and the light of man's work – imagined as the sun changing the colour of the white stone of the Museum and the glow of the building from within at night. The gardens of Vladimir Djurovic will also share a fundamental duality – that of nature "as evidence of God's creation" within an ordered plan imagined by men.

1 Written interview with Vladimir Djurovic by the
   author, 3 June 2008.
2 Ibid.
3 Interview with Vladimir Djurovic by the author,
   Paris, France, 31 January 2007.
4 Interview with His Highness the Aga Khan by the
   author, London, United Kingdom, 6 March 2007.
5 Interview with Vladimir Djurovic by the author,
   Paris, France, 31 January 2007.
6 Architects of Record for both the Ismaili Centre
   and the Aga Khan Museum.
7 Written interview with Vladimir Djurovic by the
   author, 3 June 2008.
8 E-mail from Vladimir Djurovic to the author,
   7 July 2008.
9 Vladimir Djurovic Landscape Architecture,
   'The Ismaili Centre and Aga Khan Museum, Toronto',
   pamphlet for internal use, 2007.
10 Written interview with Vladimir Djurovic by the
   author, 3 June 2008.
11 Interview with His Highness the Aga Khan by the
   author, London, United Kingdom, 6 March 2007.

MUSEUMS AND EXHIBITIONS

Although it may have appeared over time that each new initiative of His Highness the Aga Khan was destined to function independently, the overall strategy of these programmes is now quite clear. The Aga Khan Museum in Toronto is not destined to be an isolated oasis of comprehension, but rather part of a scheme to bring Islam and the West closer together, and also to provide the populations of Muslim countries with a better understanding of their own culture and civilizations. In the words of Luis Monreal, the General Manager of the Aga Khan Trust for Culture (AKTC): "In the strategy of His Highness to use the Museum as an educational tool, the Aga Khan Museum is not set up in isolation. At the same time, His Highness is creating museums in the Muslim world. Two examples are the Museum of Historic Cairo and the Indian Ocean Maritime Museum in Zanzibar."[1] Simultaneously with these initiatives, a programme of travelling exhibitions and of assistance to museums in developing countries has been launched. The first travelling exhibition concerned works from the Aga Khan Museum and was seen in 2007 and 2008 in Parma (Italy), London, Paris and Lisbon.

On a tract of land measuring thirty hectares, used for centuries as a rubbish pile, His Highness the Aga Khan undertook the creation of Azhar Park in Cairo in 1995. Inaugurated in 2004, the Park is named after the great Azhar Mosque, located slightly north of the Darb al-Ahmar area. Al-Azhar Mosque was established in 970 by Iman al-Mu'izz, the Fatimid founder of Cairo. Al-Azhar, meaning "the most flourished and shining" in Arabic, was dedicated to Sayeda Fatima al-Zahra', daughter of the Prophet

Mohammed, from whom His Highness the Aga Khan descends. It is only natural, then, that this great new Park in the heart of Cairo, close to its Fatimid roots and created by the present Aga Khan, should be called Azhar Park.

In creating this place of calm in the midst of Cairo's teeming life, His Highness the Aga Khan wrote: "We stand today confronted with starkly different visions of the future of historic cities. At a time when our heritage, the anchor of our identity and source of inspiration, is being threatened with destruction, by war and environmental degradation, by the inexorable demographic and economic pressures of exploding urban growth, or by simple neglect, there can be no doubt that it is time to act. Will we allow the wealth that is the past to be swept away, or will we assume our responsibility to defend what remains of the irreplaceable fabric of history? My answer is clear. One of our most urgent priorities must be to value, and protect, what is greatest in our common heritage. Breathing new life into the legacy of the past demands a creativity, tolerance and understanding beyond the ordinary." [2]

THE MUSEUM OF HISTORIC CAIRO, CAIRO, EGYPT

It is very much in this spirit that the AKTC is building the Museum of Historic Cairo at the north end of Azhar Park in cooperation with the Supreme Council of Antiquities of Egypt. Luis Monreal states: "The general reasons for creating this Museum are the same ones that inspired the founding of the Aga Khan Museum in Toronto. It will offer Cairene and Muslim populations that visit an informal and

An aerial view of Azhar Park in Cairo, created on the site of a former rubbish dump in the heart of the medieval city. The new Museum of Historic Cairo will be situated at the top edge of the Park as seen in this image.

effective insight into the history of Cairo. The Museum is an important educational tool because its objects have an emotional impact and do not necessarily require academic or formal education to appreciate them, at least in part. The history of Cairo is of particular interest to His Highness and the Ismaili community, given the fact that Cairo was the capital of the Fatimid Empire, the only time in history that the Shia Imami Ismailis constituted a state. Within the context of the other project created by His Highness – Azhar Park – the Museum adds a very important cultural asset to what is already an important space of leisure. This is a partnership with the Supreme Council of Antiquities of Egypt. The building and its collections are owned by the Council. What we do is to provide technical and design services to develop the project and to build the Museum. It will function as a visitor's centre, guiding tourists to sites near Azhar Park – the Fatimid remains excavated by the French archaeological mission, or the Ayyubid Wall excavated and restored by the AKTC. It will provide opportunities to discover and visit the neighbouring Darb al-Ahmar district and other neighbouring historic areas. It focuses a beacon on Islamic Cairo and its founders, the Fatimids."[3]

The 2500-square-metre Museum is thus located at the heart of the historic centre of Cairo. As the documentation of the Aga Khan Development Network (AKDN) explains: "Art and architectural elements from Heliopolis, the early settlements of Cairo and the City's major historical periods will be on show, including the Fatimid Golden Age, the periods of the Ayyubids and Mamluks, and the era of Ottoman rule.

Special rooms will recreate the atmosphere of nineteenth-century Cairo. The Museum will house some of the great wealth of the art and artefacts of Cairo's medieval heritage that is not currently on display to the public. To conserve and restore the artefacts and artworks that will be shown in the Museum, the AKTC has set up a conservation laboratory that is training young local technicians in this field. At the same time, important art and architectural elements for the Cairo Museum of Islamic Art are being restored in the same facility."[4] The Museum will be complemented by exhibition spaces within the neighbouring Ayyubid Wall and within restored cultural buildings in the historic city that visitors will be encouraged to discover, following special itineraries, as they leave the Museum.

THE INDIAN OCEAN MARITIME MUSEUM, ZANZIBAR, TANZANIA

Beginning in 1992, the Aga Khan Historic Cities Programme (HCP) undertook conservation work in the Zanzibar Stone Town area. Their work on the former Tharia Topan Jubilee Hospital, called the Old Dispensary, built beginning in 1887 in the Old Stone Town of Zanzibar, was a main element of the intervention. In 1997, the building was converted into the Stone Town Cultural Centre. It is this building that will house a two-storey museum dedicated to the Indian Ocean as a maritime space in which, since prehistory, the exchange of goods, ideas and myths has taken place between its diverse coastal civilizations. Luis Monreal explains: "The Indian Ocean Maritime Museum responds to the same global strategy but

Built as the Tharia Topan Jubilee Hospital (Zanzibar, Tanzania, 1887), this structure was restored by the Aga Khan Trust for Culture and converted into the Stone Town Cultural Centre (1997). Long called the Old Dispensary, it will be the location of the Indian Ocean Maritime Museum.

An exhibiton of the Aga Khan Museum Collection entitled *Splendori a Corte*, which took place in the Palazzo della Pilotta, in Parma, Italy, in 2007.

has other particular goals. The first is to bring Zanzibar Stone Town a new and important cultural asset that will reinforce and compliment the conservation and rehabilitation work undertaken by the AKTC and will constitute a new attraction for foreign tourists. The Museum responds to the idea of promoting tourism of quality in Zanzibar. It is aimed at people who go there more for culture than for the beaches. The Museum has succeeded in salvaging the celebrated Sultan's Barge, a nineteenth-century vessel complete with canopy, oars and gilded decoration, which will be a major attraction for visitors. The ceremonial boat was in very bad condition, abandoned in Zanzibar Harbour, but was fully restored by the AKTC. The Museum intends to show how a sea-faring culture moved through this region, linking very different material cultures of which the common denominator was the Islamic faith. The Museum will underline the pluralistic and tolerant basis of Islam. In Zanzibar, there were long-term and successful contacts between animist black Africa, Christian colonizers and the Islamic populations. The Museum will explain the origins of navigation along the coast ranging back to the pre-Islamic stories of the Indian Ocean. It will be an asset for local education as well. The main thrust is always education."[5]

Information about the evolution of Arab navigation and the travels of Ibn Battuta, Marco Polo, Ibn Majid, or Zheng He will be part of the exhibitions. Pirates and trading companies, the slave trade and cloves are all part of the fascinating history of Zanzibar. According to the AKDN description: "Models of naval vessels,

old navigation instruments and maps and other original artefacts that illustrate the history of the commercial and cultural contacts between Africa, the Middle East, the Indian subcontinent and the Far East will be featured. Indian Ocean ecology and the effects of human activity on local ecosystems will also be highlighted in interactive models and displays."[6]

TRAVELLING EXHIBITIONS

The Aga Khan Museum in Toronto will initiate or participate in three to four major temporary exhibitions per year concerning the Islamic world, presented in historic, geographic or thematic terms. The first major travelling show organized by the AKTC and the Museum grouped together a number of the most significant works of the Aga Khan Museum Collections and toured to Parma (Italy), London, the Louvre in Paris and the Calouste Gulbenkian Museum in Lisbon.[7] The institutions involved in these shows may well engage in future collaboration with the Aga Khan Museum, but in the meantime the 170 miniatures, manuscripts, ceramics and other artworks displayed in London, for example, give the clearest idea of the objects that will form the core of the institution. As His Highness the Aga Khan wrote in the forward for the catalogue of the London exhibition: "This exhibition of masterpieces from the Islamic world underlines that the arts, particularly when they are spiritually inspired, can become a medium of discourse that transcends the barriers of our day-to-day experiences and preoccupations. Many questions are currently being raised in the

Above and right, images from the exhibition entitled *The Path of Princes: Masterpieces of Islamic Art from the Aga Khan Museum Collection*, at the Calouste Gulbenkian Foundation, Lisbon, Portugal, in 2008.

West about the Muslim world, with countless misconceptions and misunderstandings occurring between our contemporary societies. I thus hope that this exhibition will hold a special significance at a time which calls for enlightened encounters amongst faiths and cultures."[8]

The London exhibition included such masterpieces as a Qur'an folio in gold kufic script on blue parchment (North Africa, 9th–10th century, AKM 00477). Although the contents of the Aga Khan Museum are not based on a collection formed over the centuries, there is a relationship between this thousand-year-old parchment and the history of the Shia Imami Ismailis. His Highness the Aga Khan writes: "The arts have always had a special significance for my family. More than a thousand years ago, my ancestors, the Fatimid Imams, encouraged patronage of the arts and fostered the creation of collections of outstanding works of art and libraries of rare and significant manuscripts. Many of my family members are art lovers and collectors. In particular my late uncle, Prince Sadruddin Aga Khan, was a great connoisseur of manuscripts and miniatures, and many of the works on paper and parchment presented in this exhibition came from his collection."[9] Another work from the collections, *Rustam Pursues the Div Akvan Disguised as an Onager* (Folio

294r from the *Shahnameh* of Shah Tahmasp, Iran, Tabriz, *c.* 1530–35, AKM 00162), shows not only the highest quality in Islamic art, but also its variety, here delving into a figurative and lush fantasy world that might seem far removed from a folio of the Qur'an. And yet it is precisely Islam that unites these works, though they may be separated by centuries and hundreds or even thousands of kilometres in their point of origin. It is an indication of the level of the collection that the itinerary of this exhibition took it to the Louvre in Paris and the Calouste Gulbenkian Museum in Lisbon. As in all other initiatives, His Highness the Aga Khan has seen to it that the study and display of his works is carried out in the best circumstances possible. Though scholars and collectors have devoted their lives to understanding and possessing such works, they were offered in the travelling exhibition of the Aga Khan Museum to the view of all those with the desire to know more about Islamic art. Even without the capacity to read Arabic or knowledge of the legends of sixteenth-century Iran, it is clear to the visitor that a deep and varied culture has produced these works. That realization might indeed be the first step to understanding that can encourage the very tolerance that His Highness the Aga Khan has long sought to foster.

1 Interview with Luis Monreal by the author, Geneva, Switzerland, 10 June 2008.
2 His Highness the Aga Khan, 'Introduction', *Cairo, Revitalising a Historic Metropolis*, Umberto Allemandi & Co., Turin/Aga Khan Trust for Culture, Geneva, 2004.
3 Interview with Luis Monreal by the author, Geneva, Switzerland, 10 June 2008.
4 See: http://www.akdn.org/agency/aktc_museum.html#iomm, accessed on 5 July 2008.
5 Interview with Luis Monreal by the author, Geneva, Switzerland, 10 June 2008.
6 See: http://www.akdn.org/agency/aktc_museum.html#iomm, accessed on 5 July 2008.
7 *Splendori a Corte*, Palazzo della Pilotta, Parma, Italy, 31 March to 3 June 2007; *Spirit & Life*, The Ismaili Centre, London, United Kingdom, 14 July to 31 August 2007; *Chefs-d'œuvre islamiques de l'Aga Khan Museum*, Louvre, Paris, France, 5 October 2007 to 7 January 2008; *The Path of Princes*, Calouste Gulbenkian Museum, Lisbon, Portugal, 14 March to 6 July 2008.
8 His Highness the Aga Khan, 'Forward', *Spirit & Life, Masterpieces of Islamic Art from the Aga Khan Museum Collections*, Aga Khan Trust for Culture, Geneva, 2007.
9 Ibid.

Another image from the exhibition entitled *The Path of Princes: Masterpeices of Islamic Art from the Aga Khan Museum Collection*, at the Calouste Gulbenkian Foundation, Lisbon, Portugal, in 2008.

The Aga Khan Museum, Toronto

FEASIBILITY STUDIES: Sasaki Associates, Boston, Massachusetts, United States
DESIGN ARCHITECTS: Fumihiko Maki and Maki and Associates, Tokyo, Japan
ARCHITECT OF RECORD: Moriyama & Teshima Architects, Toronto, Canada
LANDSCAPE ARCHITECTS: Vladimir Djurovic Landscape Architecture (VDLA), Beirut, Lebanon

The author would like to thank Shiraz Allibhai and William O'Reilly (AKTC), Gary Kamemoto (Maki and Associates), and Sally Farroukh and Mira Sadik (VDLA) for their invaluable assistance in the course of the preparation of this book.

Picture Credits

Courtesy of Aga Khan Trust for Culture pp. 1, 2, 4, 16, 18, 19, 22, 23, 30, 31, 32, 33, 34, 46, 47, 51, 58, 61, 65, 66, 67, 68, 70, 71, 73, 80, 88, 91, 103, 105, 106, 108, 109, 111
Gul Chotrani p. 60
Courtesy of Charles Correa Associates p. 38
Courtesy of Vladimir Djurovic Landscape Architecture (VDLA), Beirut, Lebanon pp. 13, 14, 24, 27, 28, 29, 40, 44, 82, 83, 84, 86, 87, 92, 95, 96, 97, 99, 100, 101, cover
Tor Eigeland/Saudi Aramco World/PADIA pp. 26, 94
Courtesy of Imara (Wynford Drive) Limited pp. 21, 39
Toshiharu Kitajima p. 48
Courtesy of Fumihiko Maki and Maki Associates, Tokyo, Japan pp. 12, 17, 20, 25, 35, 36, 37, 42, 43, 49, 50, 52, 53, 54, 55, 56, 59, 62, 63, 64, 72, 74, 76, 77, 78, 79
Luis Monreal p. 11
Moriyama & Teshima pp. 45, 75
Gary Otte p. 89

Imprint

© Prestel Verlag, Munich · Berlin · London · New York, 2008
© Aga Khan Trust for Culture, 2008
© for the artworks, by the architects, artists, their heirs or assigns

Front cover: A computer rendering by Vladimir Djurovic Landscape Architecture shows the gardens and reflecting pools between the Aga Khan Museum by Fumihiko Maki (right) and the Ismaili Centre by Charles Correa (left). © Courtesy of Vladimir Djurovic Landscape Architecture, Beirut

p. 2: **Mother-of-Pearl Shell Engraved with Verses from the Qur'an,** India or Turkey, 18th century (diameter: 14.5 cm; AKM 00665)

p. 4: **Pottery Albarello, or Pharmacy Jar (detail),** Syria, late 14th or early 15th century (height: 31.7 cm; AKM 00569)

Library of Congress Control Number is available; British Library Cataloguing-in-Publication Data: a catalogue record for this book is available from the British Library; Deutsche Nationalbibliothek holds a record of this publication in the Deutsche Nationalbibliografie; detailed bibliographical data can be found under: "http://dnb.ddb.de" http://dnb.ddb.de.

Prestel books are available worldwide. Please contact your nearest bookseller or one of the above addresses for information concerning your local distributor.

PRESTEL VERLAG
Königinstrasse 9
80539 Munich
Tel. +49 (0)89 24 29 08-300
Fax +49 (0)89 24 29 08-335
www.prestel.de

PRESTEL PUBLISHING LTD.
4 Bloomsbury Place
London WC1A 2QA
Tel. +44 (0)20 7323-5004
Fax +44 (0)20 7636-8004

PRESTEL PUBLISHING
900 Broadway, Suite 603
New York, NY 10003
Tel. +1 (212) 995-2720
Fax +1 (212) 995-2733
www.prestel.com

PROJECT MANAGEMENT: Anja Paquin
PRODUCTION: Simone Zeeb
DESIGN COORDINATION: Cilly Klotz
COPY-EDITING: Harriet Graham, Turin
DESIGN AND LAYOUT: SOFAROBOTNIK, Augsburg & Munich
PRE-PRESS PRODUCTION: Reproline mediateam, Munich
PRINTING AND BINDING: TBB, Banská Bystrica

Printed on acid-free paper.

ISBN 978-3-7913-6210-6 (English museum edition)
ISBN 978-3-7913-4146-0 (English trade edition)
ISBN 978-3-7913-4147-7 (French museum edition)